Golf Begins at Forty

Sam Snead

Golf Begins at Forty

with
Dick Aultman

with illustrations
by
James McQueen

The
Dial Press
New York

Published by
The Dial Press
1 Dag Hammarskjold Plaza
New York, New York 10017

Manufactured in the United States of America

Third Printing—1982

Library of Congress Cataloging in Publication Data

Snead, Samuel.
Golf begins at forty.

Includes index.
1. Golf. I. Aultman, Dick, joint author.
II. Title.
GV965.S664   796.352′3   78-5601
ISBN 0-8037-2850-6

Contents

Golf Begins
at Forty

Introduction

Before Dick Aultman and I sat down and actually started working on this book, we decided on one basic guideline.

We agreed that it should be truly for the over-forty player—man or woman—rather than a standard golfing text, thinly disguised with a few allusions to playing the game later in life.

Thus this book does not cover the golfing waterfronts. Instead, it presents solutions only for those problems that are especially pertinent to the older player, such as loss of distance, reduced flexibility, physical and mental tension, fatigue, self-defeating attitudes, and so on.

It covers the problems and offers cures, but it also tells the older player how better to utilize those advantages he or she may have over the younger golfer, such as additional experience and, perhaps, additional time to play, practice or simply to sit back and reflect.

No doubt many golfers over forty will feel that they do not yet need instruction tailored to combat the effects of advancing age. Quite frankly, I would have felt the same way when I was in my forties. Looking back, however, I now realize that it is never too early to start developing certain swing habits and certain attitudes toward the game that will offset the problems to come. Believe me, your swing isn't going to get any longer and freer in the years ahead, and it's a whole lot easier to start to adjust to that at forty-five than at fifty-five.

Because our basic guideline was to make this book truly for the older player, we also agreed that it had to be somewhat unique in at least one other way. Unlike many other instruction books, this one does not require a major overhaul of the reader's entire swing. It is not a "method" book. Though I do stress a correct grip, because no golfer of any age can play consistently well without one, I do not insist that the reader change everything else to fit a certain model.

The older golfer can learn new tricks, and this book tells how. I believe, however, that most experienced players should improve and build on the swing they have developed. For most it would be a waste of time and energy—probably more harmful than productive—to attempt to completely alter their swing pattern without a professional teacher on hand for face-to-face guidance.

Because this book does not detail a specific swing method, I think you will find it relatively easy to understand and quite simple to apply. The chapters are purposely short, the instruction message in each is designed to be clear and to the point.

I start off each chapter with an anecdote from my playing or teaching experience. One reason I've done this is to make the book more fun to read. The main reason, however, is to make the instruction that follows easier to understand and remember.

The book is divided into three main sections. The first—"Getting More from What You've Got"—includes chapters that stress ways you can score better without actually changing your technique. It also tells you how to decide what needs changing, and how to make your efforts—through practice—more rewarding.

The second section describes the things that I feel most golfers over forty should consider doing with their full swings. The third section deals with ways to improve your short shots, especially your putting.

I feel I am qualified to do this book for golfers over forty. Most of the people I play with these days—and most of those I've taught over the years—are well past that age. I've seen the problems they face. I've come to understand how they can best be helped. I've learned which changes they can handle physically, and which they cannot. I've come to understand their attitudes.

And I feel that I've personally experienced the special problems that older golfers face. I've fought the same battles—the shortening of my swing arc, the tendency to yip putts, an occasional loss of rhythm, the fear of losing distance—and the bad habits that this can create—and the aches and pains that come with increasing frequency.

I've learned to cope with these things and you can too. In many ways my golf game really did improve after I passed my fortieth—even my fiftieth—birthday. Today, at sixty-five, I'm still finding new ways to score, on occasion, as well as I ever could—sometimes even better. I sincerely hope that this book will help you do the same.

Sam Snead
August 26, 1977

one

Getting More From
What You've Got

1

Use Your Keys to Unlock Tension

One day a few years ago I was sitting at a table with two of golf's all-time fine players, Dr. Cary Middlecoff and Paul Runyan. We were talking about what goes into making a great golfer.

Both Cary and Paul agreed that hard work—countless hours of practice—was a necessary ingredient. However, they disagreed somewhat on the relative importance of physical capability and intelligence.

Paul, being a small man, has fought an uphill battle all his life to gain more distance on his shots. And he's succeeded. Today, at seventy, he drives the ball farther than he ever did during his prime in the 1930s when he won two PGA Championships.

Still, Paul feels that his success has been limited by his physique, so naturally he believes—and I agree—that innate physical capabilities play a large part in one's golfing success.

"Now you take Sam here," Runyan, who has always been extremely candid, said to Middlecoff. "Here's a man that was born with all the natural ability in the world. He became a great golfer largely because of that ability. However, I can't imagine the additional success he would have achieved if he'd had the intelligence to go along with all that natural talent."

Then Middlecoff answered with something that I think is pertinent to all golfers, but especially to the older player.

"You're right about Sam's natural ability," he said to Runyan, "but I can't go along with his lacking intelligence. Sam's always been smart enough to know that the surest way to ruin his swing would be to start getting too complex about it. He's kept his thinking simple, and he's done it on purpose. I think that's where he's really been intelligent."

Actually, I've thought about my golf swing and fiddled around with it a whole lot more than people realize. But Doc's point is certainly valid. The surest way I know to mess up on the golf course is to go out there and start thinking about a whole bunch of things while you're swinging the club.

All that does is bind you up. All that thinking gets you physically tense. Muscles tighten. Swings get shorter and faster. The ball goes everywhere, but not where you hoped it would.

My advice to older golfers especially is to keep things simple up there in your head. That's the best way to make those old bones and muscles function smoothly, and correctly.

When you're getting along in years, why start taking apart your golfing engine piece by piece? It just might take the rest of your days, and then some, to put all the parts back together again. In the meantime you'll be sputtering around the course with half your pistons and spark plugs still back in the garage.

I don't mean that you shouldn't continually strive to improve. I certainly feel that older golfers should continue to practice as much as they possibly can. What I am saying is that you should avoid ruining all the good things you've learned to do in golf over the years by taking your game in for a major overhaul.

There is a time to work on various parts of your swing, to refine different moves and positions. You should do that when you are practicing. That's also the time to experiment.

However, when you actually go on the course to play golf, you'd better weed out all that thinking and settle on just one or two thoughts for the day.

That's what I do, always have and always will. Ideally I try to play in sort of a daze as far as my swing is concerned. I try merely to settle on what type of shot I want to hit; visualize it beforehand; sense how it will feel to make it, and then let it all happen.

But sometimes I need to think about something in my swing as I swing, especially when I'm not hitting the ball too well. That's where my "keys" come into the picture. My keys are a few simple thoughts that I have developed over the years. Each key has a certain purpose. Each triggers a whole bunch of other things to happen. Each key, in the end, affects my shots a certain way.

I might stick with the same key for several rounds. Then gradually my shots will start misbehaving. Usually that means I've overdone that key.

So then I take up a different key to offset the problem that's starting to develop. I might switch to this new key in the middle of a round. I can do this with confidence because I know what it will do to my shots.

I'm not going to tell you what my keys are because they probably wouldn't work for you. They might foul you up because your swing is different from mine, or because you might apply the wrong key at the wrong time, or the wrong way. Everyone has to find their own personal keys.

It's really quite simple to do. Merely take note of each thing you find that corrects a specific type of bad shot.

For instance, let's say you're starting to slice your drives. You take a lesson to correct that problem, or you work it out for yourself. You might find that your drives quit slicing whenever you hold the club with an extremely light grip pressure in your right hand. Or you might find that it helps to align your shoulders more to the right when you address the ball. Or maybe the thought of making a longer backswing corrects the problem.

Whatever key you happen to come up with will be your key against slicing. Actually, you might find two or three different keys. In any case, make a list of your keys and study that list every once in a while. In time you'll have one or two keys to take care of any problem that might start developing in your game.

Be sure to keep your keys simple: a light grip pressure; a certain

positioning of the ball in your stance; a slow takeaway of the clubhead from the ball; a gradual acceleration of your left arm through the hitting area. Keep them simple, and specific.

I think you should practice these various keys one at a time. Don't mix them up in the same swing, especially when you're playing on the course. One key to a swing is about all that our minds can handle.

The more confident you become about your keys, the less you'll tense up when things start going bad. Golf is supposed to be relaxing, so work with your keys. Save all that brainpower for projects where it really does some good.

Practicing—
How, What and Why

Some folks seem to think that I woke up one morning as a youngster, made myself a golf club out of a swamp maple tree—leaving on some bark for better gripping—and immediately started belting out 250-yard drives, straight and true.

I only wish that were the case. It sure would have been nice if some golfing god had, in fact, handed me a "natural" swing that never went haywire.

If it had happened that way, I probably wouldn't have been sitting with a friend a few years back, trying to figure out how many shots I'd hit over the past forty-odd years, developing my so-called natural swing.

We decided on 1,600,040.

By now I'm probably over 2,000,000.

In golf, you get out of it what you put into it. Most people won't put much into it.

The golf swing is mainly something that's learned—a habit you must acquire. Acquiring it is hard work; at least it was for me. Maintaining it is just as hard.

Especially when you get older. Most older golfers are like older fighters. The older a fighter gets, the less he wants to work out. He'll take shortcuts in training. The next thing you know, he's been clobbered.

Most older golfers have more time to practice than they did when they were younger. But gradually they find other things to enjoy. Then they fret because their handicaps creep upward faster and faster.

"But I play two or three times a week," they'll say.

Fine. If you play quite a bit, you won't need so much practice. But everyone should practice. Even just a little effort, in the right direction, can make a great difference in your average score. Here are the directions I think you should take when you do, hopefully, go to work on your game.

First, practice frequently in short doses. I'd rather see the older player put in, say, a half-hour session four, five or more times a week, rather than one exhausting marathon workout that leaves both him and his swing sputtering on just two or three cylinders. Never practice beyond the point of feeling tired, or bored.

Second, practice like you play. Some people spend a lifetime learning to make wonderful swings, but never seem to improve their scoring all that much. It's fine to practice your swing—certain moves and certain positions—but eventually you should get around to practicing shotmaking. That means picking targets that you can easily reach, and then trying to make each shot either land or finish on that spot.

Third, to get the most possible good from your practicing, emphasize fundamentals. These are the basic things from which all other good things evolve. For instance, instead of working for hours to develop precisely correct wrist action at various stages of your swing, merely develop a sound grip that will let such wrist action happen automatically. Instead of spending months learning to swing the club on a proper path and a correct plane, simply master an address position—body alignment and posture—that will create such a swing path and plane. Or, if pace and rhythm are your problems, perhaps a lighter grip and a slower takeaway will be the simplest and quickest ways to solve the whole matter.

Many readers may not have enough understanding to know which basic, fundamental cause is producing all the undesirable effects. If this is your problem, ask a professional instructor to look at your swing.

Ask him or her to prescribe cures for the basic faults, rather than for the various problems that result from them.

Fourth, practice your short game. It takes far less time and effort to putt and chip than to make full swings, yet the rewards—in terms of lower scoring—usually come sooner.

My final word about practice is that it's the only way I know to build true confidence in your ability and trust in your equipment. I believe that older golfers, especially, need all the confidence they can possibly develop.

Warm Up
Those Old Joints

Late in the summer of 1936, I heard that the touring pros were to play in a $5,000 tournament in Hershey, Pennsylvania. I'd saved a few dollars I'd won in some local tournaments, so I decided to drive up there and check out all those big-name players, like Gene Sarazen, Leo Diegel, Paul Runyan and Horton Smith.

I left home at night and drove all the way—a little over 300 miles—in my V-8 Ford. I finally found the course, just as a group of three players I didn't know were teeing off for their practice round.

I walked up to the group and asked to make sure that this was where they were having the tournament. They said it was. One of the men, who turned out to be George Fazio, invited me to join them. The others started walking down the fairway, but he waited at the tee while I rushed back to the car and changed my shoes.

I was excited about playing with the big boys, and I had to rush to join them. Naturally I didn't have time to hit any practice shots. Also, after fighting that steering wheel all night my arms felt as tight as banjo strings.

The first hole at Hershey Country Club was about 345 yards long with a hill running down from the front of the tee. There was a sewage plant near the bottom of it and a factory off to the right.

With all that tension and rushing, I teed up my ball and gave it a swing that must have been faster than a hummingbird in heat. I topped the shot. It dribbled down the hill into the sewage area—obviously unplayable.

My next try sliced wildly off to the right, somewhere into the factory.

I was so embarrassed by then that I felt like running back to my car and heading home to mother. However, Fazio, a real gentleman, sort of soothed me down.

"Hit another one, son," he said in a kindly tone.

This time I took a deep breath, gripped the club lightly and tried to make a full, smooth swing. The club felt real good when it hit the ball.

"Where'd it go?" Fazio asked.

One of the other men, down the fairway, yelled back: "My God, he's on the green."

Fazio just stared at me, sort of dazed.

On the second hole there's a creek that runs across the fairway. Fazio said it was about 275 yards out. He told me that everyone played an iron off the tee so they'd finish short of the water.

I took out my driver and flew the ball over the hazard.

"Boy," he said, "I haven't seen any drives like that one lately."

I kept it up the rest of the day. On the third hole—about 600 yards—I was over the green on my second shot.

When it was all over I'd shot 67. I felt real good because now I knew I could keep up with the pros. But I still wished I hadn't wasted those shots on the first tee.

I never want to rush myself into a round of golf. I was lucky at Hershey, coming back like I did after those first two drives. But then I was only twenty-four. My body could stand the strain of hitting full-out drives without any sort of warm-up. Today I'd be lucky if they didn't have to cart me off to the hospital and cement me into a body cast.

As we get older it becomes more and more important to prepare our minds and bodies for playing golf. The older golfer should never tee up without first hitting at least a small bucket of practice balls.

A pre-round warm-up not only preserves your body from having something tear or come loose; it also helps eliminate those high scores on the early holes. Why ruin your enjoyment of the day just because you didn't allow yourself an extra twenty minutes or so to get ready?

Before a round of golf I like to take things slow and easy. I give myself enough time to drive slowly to the course. That way I can hold the steering wheel lightly and build up a nice soft feeling in my hands and fingers.

I'll probably do some daydreaming as I drive. I'll think about how I'll play those first few holes. I'll imagine my drives finishing in perfect position. I'll see my approach shots finishing up close to the hole—never more than five or six feet away. I never miss the putt.

By the time I get to the course I'm all soothed down to make some nice smooth swings, and I've got my mind tuned in to golf.

I'll start my pre-round practice sessions by hitting a few pitch shots with my wedge, just to get loose and feel the pace of my swing. Then I gradually work into the longer clubs—8-iron, 6-iron, 4-iron, 2-iron, 3-wood—hitting just a few shots with each, finishing with the driver. Finally, I'll hit a few chip shots and putts at the practice green, just to make sure I've got a good touch for distance and a nice rhythm to my stroke.

I'll try not to do a lot of fiddling with my swing during pre-round practice. If my shots are not going just right, I may pick out one key thought that will straighten things out. That will be my thought for the day. But I try not to get too technical about my swing at this point. Mainly I want to simply loosen up and keep my head clear.

If you find your pre-round shots aren't so good, just keep swinging as fully and as smoothly as you can. Hold the club lightly. Usually, poor pre-round shots simply come from not yet being fully warmed up.

If your shots still continue to bend off-line, don't panic. Figure that on the course you'll simply allow for any slicing or hooking tendency you might find developing. You'll merely aim to offset the shot you've been getting in practice.

I think everyone should develop their own pre-round routine to find out what works best for them. For instance, I don't hit nearly as many shots before a round these days as I did when I was younger. I've

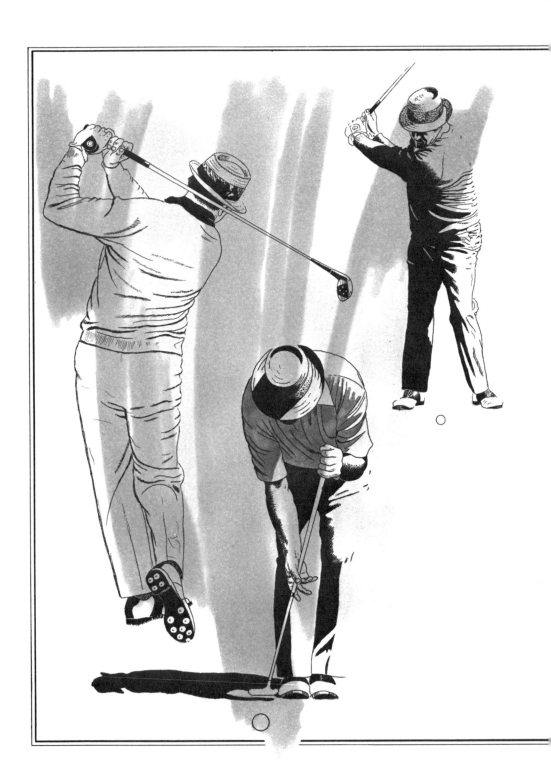

found that overdoing my pre-round workout comes back to haunt me later in the day. My first clue came when I realized that my second-nine scores were invariably higher than those on the front nine.

There are another couple of things I'd like to warn older players about, regarding their pre-round habits.

First, don't go out to play with a lot of food in your stomach. Whenever I see someone having a big lunch before our game, I figure I can safely up the ante on our bets. Digesting all that food drains you of energy. You won't swing as well as you should, and you won't be as alert mentally. You'll feel sort of listless. You'll find yourself making stupid decisions.

Second, I've come to realize that caffeine is one of the worst things for your nerves. Older players who tend to get a little jumpy anyway surely don't need any additional stimulant.

I really love my couple of cups of coffee in the morning. I grew up on the stuff; my mother fed us bread dipped in coffee when we were babies. But I know it's bad for my golf. Recently I heard that the caffeine in one cup of coffee stays with you for 12 to 16 hours, so I'm swearing off for good. It's too darn expensive anyway.

See Success
Before You Swing

Many years ago I was standing on the first tee at Augusta National, waiting for my turn to tee off in the Masters tournament.

My playing partner for that day was the late Jim Turnesa, a fine golfer who later went on to win the PGA Championship in 1952.

As I waited, I watched Turnesa play his drive. I mean I really studied every move he made. I watched him set up to the ball, waggle his club and then swing. I watched his ball fly through the air, a high shot far to the right. I watched the ball disappear deep into a grove of trees.

Then it was my turn. Sure enough, I hit exactly the same drive, a high push to the right. My ball landed in the trees in almost exactly the same spot.

That's when I quit studying other people's shots. Now I watch just casually, if at all.

The reason my drive duplicated Turnesa's was that I'd given my mind such a vivid picture of his swing and his ball in flight. The human mind is a wonderful computer, but it sure can backfire if you give it a negative thought. So often you think about making a bad shot and that's exactly what your mind makes your body produce. What you see is what you get.

Leo Diegel, a two-time PGA Championship winner, knew this all too well. One year Leo fell into some bad thinking about the first drive he would have to hit in the Los Angeles Open at Riviera Country Club.

The first hole at Riviera has an out of bounds to the left of the fairway. There were some horse stables over there. For weeks before the tournament, Leo kept imagining his first drive flying into those stables. It became an obsession.

This kept up during his practice rounds before the tournament. He'd put his tee shot into the stable area every time.

Well, Leo finally solved his problem, more or less. On the first day of the tournament he stepped up to that tee shot and actually aimed for the horse barns. He purposely hit the ball out of bounds, took his penalty and teed up another ball.

"That takes care of that," he muttered. "Now I can start playing golf."

When golfers get older, they seem to build up more and more mental tension. This mental tension becomes physical tension. The last thing older folks need is more tension in those muscles that are already starting to lose some of their flexibility.

I'm sure that a lot of this tension comes from seeing bad shots before they happen. You watch a youngster putt. He just steps up there and bangs it into the cup, clear and simple. He drops those putts merely because he knows that's what he is supposed to do. Unlike the veteran player, the youngster hasn't had time to be brainwashed. He hasn't had a chance to start learning about—and thinking about—all the terrible things that might happen if he misses the shot. He doesn't give his mind a picture of a missed shot. Instead he sees success, and that's often what he gets, because he's shown his mind what to make his body do.

The older golfer has a huge inventory of past shots, both good and bad. He's seen long, straight drives that have rolled forever. But he's also seen tee shots that have dribbled along the fairway or sliced out of bounds. He's seen long putts curl down a slope and drop into the cup. He's also seen 2-footers slide around the rim and stay out.

So the older player has a choice. He can either see a good shot before he plays it, or he can see a disaster. I've found that the clearer the image I can produce of a good shot, the better my chances are of making it happen.

I actually see the ball in flight before I ever choose my club and set up to the shot. I see it going to my target. I see it landing on the fairway and bouncing and rolling forward. Or I see it landing on the green and, maybe, taking a bounce and then spinning backward to the flagstick.

Then I sort of sense how my swing should feel to make the shot that I've visualized. That's another thing older people can learn to do. Why? Because they have made similar shots before, and they've felt themselves making them.

I'm not saying that this sort of positive thinking comes easy. If you haven't done it too much before, it will take some training to see good shots before you play them. The more you do it, however, the easier it gets.

You won't make the shot you've visualized every time. Maybe you won't make it one time out of ten. What will happen, though, is that most of the time your mis-hit shots won't be quite so badly mis-hit. You'll make better swings and better putting strokes because you've given your computer a positive image of what you're trying to achieve. That alone has got to improve your scores.

5

A Mature Outlook on Club Selection

One year I was playing in the Sam Snead Festival tournament, a pro-am event at the Greenbrier. My amateur partner was the late Paul Shields, a wonderful gentleman who was board chairman at the Pratt-Whitney Corporation.

Paul was getting along in years and he'd had two cataract operations on his eyes, but he was still an excellent competitor.

On the front nine Paul was hitting the ball pretty well, but he was always coming up short on his approach shots to the green. Finally I thought I had a solution. I got his caddie off to one side.

"Look," I said. "Whenever Mr. Shields has a shot to the green, I want you to ask him what club he wants. If he says 7-iron, give him a 6. If he says 6-iron, give him the 5. Always give him one more club than he asks for."

The caddie looked at me and shook his head.

"Can't do that, Mr. Sam—no way. He's the boss. If he found out, he'd run my tail off the course."

Finally, I decided to take matters into my own hands. We were on the 10th hole—a par-4—and I saw that Paul had a 7-iron in his hand for his second shot.

"Paul," I asked, "do you want to win this tournament?"

"Hell yes!"

"Then will you please put that club away and go with your 4-iron?"

Paul looked at me like I'd just picked his pocket.

"My God, Sam, I'll knock it clear over the green."

"Try it," I pleaded. "If you put it in jail, I'll still make a four, maybe a three."

Paul finally agreed. He put that 4-iron shot about ten feet from the hole. Then he dropped the putt for a birdie-3. With his handicap stroke, he'd given us a net-two for the hole.

Paul let me do his club selecting for the rest of the round. Sometimes I gave him three or four clubs more than he thought he should use. Each time he accepted my advice. Almost every time he finished in birdie range. We won the tournament going away.

Later I told Paul Shields some things about club selection that I'd like to tell all golfers, especially older players.

First, I explained to him that he was basing his choice of clubs on the distances that he'd hit his shots thirty years ago. It was a bitter pill, but Paul swallowed it gracefully. I know it helped him score better and enjoy the game more during his later years.

The second point I made was that almost all golfers tend to underclub themselves on most of their shots. I'd say that the normal amateur player picks the wrong club about twelve times per round on average. Almost always he finishes short of target, unless he skulls or hooks the shot and it runs forever.

The problem stems from the fact that everyone expects to hit every shot with their Sunday punch. How often do they get their Sunday punch? I'd guess one time out of ten, if they're lucky.

I find that the problem of underclubbing is even greater among older golfers. Not only do they still expect their Sunday punch, but they also resist giving in to any loss of yardage that sometimes goes with aging. It's an ego problem, and I suppose it's understandable, but good scoring in golf depends on a realistic attitude. Until you can find a way to retrieve lost length on your shots, you'd better adjust accordingly in your club selection.

Personally, I don't care what club I use so long as it does the job. It doesn't do me any good to walk off the course and tell someone I used an 8-iron on such and such hole so he will think I'm a long knocker. That doesn't enter my mind. The only thing that impresses me is a good shot, and a good score.

Recently I was playing in the PGA Seniors at Disneyworld. On this one hole I was less than a hundred yards from the flagstick, but there was a hard wind into my face. I figured I could probably reach the target with an 8-iron or 9-iron if I swung full-out. I also knew, however, that the more force I gave the shot the higher it would backspin up into that wind.

So I chose a 6-iron and beat the shot down into the wind. That ball flew up there—I'd swear it was past the hole at one time—and then it quivered and shook like one of those hawks you see. Finally it settled down on the front of the green, just over the bunker.

I suppose a lot of people would laugh at Snead hitting a 6-iron on a shot that's under a hundred yards. Who cares? I say let 'em chuckle, just so long as I'm the one who collects.

I've always been able to hit the ball pretty far—still can. I could still jump on a 7-iron and make it go 170 or 175, but I don't. I'd much rather use more club because I know that then I'll make a smoother swing. You will too.

To show you what I mean, here are the clubs I will usually use for shots of given distances under normal conditions—a clear shot, normal lie, normal pin placement, no wind. You might not find the yardages all that impressive even when compared with your own distances—but perhaps you need to think a bit about how many times you finish short of the flagstick.

100 yards and under—wedge.	166–177—5-iron.
100–120—9-iron.	178–189—4-iron.
121–138—8-iron.	190–200—3-iron.
139–152—7-iron.	201–210—2-iron.
153–165—6-iron.	210–220—1-iron.

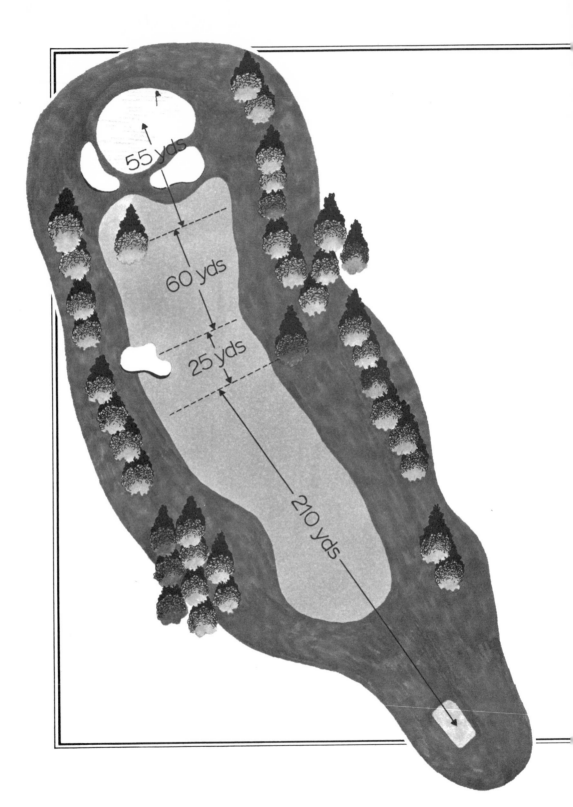

55 yds

60 yds

25 yds

210 yds

On approach shots over 220 yards I'll generally use my 3-wood, since I don't carry a 4-wood or 2-wood. Since this club is extra-long—43½ inches—I can make shots of 2-wood or 4-wood distance simply by gripping near the end or well down on the shaft.

If you cannot make up a similar type of list for the lengths that you hit with each of your clubs, then I urge that you do some measuring of your shots.

Take a yardstick out of the closet and spend a few minutes finding out how big a step you need to span it from end to end. Then, in the future, whenever you hit an average shot with a given club, pace off the distance it traveled. Keep doing this for a few rounds and you'll soon have a realistic set of measurements of your current distances. With this knowledge you can start playing golf like I do—by the numbers.

There was a time when I relied pretty much solely on my eyes to tell me what club I should use. I don't know if my eyes are still what they used to be, but I do know that I feel much more confident now that I choose my clubs, whenever possible, on the basis of specific yardage. I can't always do this when I play a course for the first time, unless it has bushes or trees placed a given distance—usually 150 yards—from the center of the green. However, I do measure yardages from given spots—bunkers, bushes, sprinkler heads, etc.—to the greens whenever I play a course before a tournament.

There is no reason why you can't do the same thing at your home club.

One thing to remember, however, is that measurements shown on the scorecard are usually made from the center of the tee, or from some marker or post embedded thereby, to the center of the green. The line of measurement is as the crow would fly along the course architect's intended line of play.

Don't forget to add or subtract yards if the tee markers and/or the flagstick itself are set behind or in front of these spots.

When playing a strange course, I find it helps to walk some fifteen or twenty paces ahead of my ball and look at the scene from there. This perspective gives you a better idea of where the flagstick sets on the green. It also makes you aware of any hidden depressions along the way that might make the shot look shorter than it really is.

Be sure to consider the wind. Even a very slight breeze can take a bunch of yards off your shots, especially those you make with the more-lofted clubs, which tend to put a lot of extra backspin on the ball.

Also remember that shots to a lowered or raised green will carry farther or shorter, respectively, than normal. Use less club to lowered greens, more to those that are raised.

Of course the best way to assure proper club selection is to follow the example of a member, now deceased, at the Seminole Golf Club in North Palm Beach, Florida.

This man liked to play for high stakes, and the real breadwinner in his bag was the 6-wood. He knew exactly how far he could hit shots with that club. I mean he knew within INCHES.

Before each round he would drive his golf cart onto the course, stopping at each par-3 hole along the way. There he'd simply pick up the tee markers and move them into a new position, exactly his 6-wood distance from the flagstick.

Play the Shot
You've Made Before

I suppose I'll go to my grave being known as the best golfer who never won our biggest championship, the U.S. Open.

Some will say that Snead couldn't handle the pressure, but that's not true. In 1937, at Oakland Hills near Detroit, I'd finished with a 283 total and everyone in the locker room came up to congratulate me. Then Ralph Guldahl rolled in from nowhere with 281, a record score. Suddenly the place felt like Death Row.

Ten years later, at St. Louis Country Club, I needed a curving, downhill 18-footer on the final green to tie Lew Worsham at 282. With Worsham and about 20,000 other folks watching, I made that putt. I lost the playoff, 69–70, but not because of the pressure.

I won the Masters in 1949 by coming from eight shots behind, shooting 67–67 in a biting wind the last two days. Five years later I beat Ben Hogan 70–71 in a playoff for my third title at Augusta.

Everyone chokes to some degree sometime, and I've had my share of those weak moments. However, I really can't blame pressure for failing to win the Open. There were other factors that were more important—perhaps some bad luck, for sure some bad golf.

And inexperience.

I was only in my third year as a touring pro when we played the

Open at Spring Mill outside Philadelphia in 1939. With only two holes remaining, I needed only two pars for a 281 total, Guldahl's record score. I figured those two pars would put me on top of the golfing world.

On the first of those two holes I overshot the green on my approach. The ball finished in thick clover. I chipped out five feet short of the hole. My putt for the par missed by an inch.

On the final tee we waited what seemed like hours while officials cleared the gallery from the fairway. During that time I kept telling myself that I needed a birdie-4 on that 558-yard hole.

As it turned out a par-5 would have been sufficient. A bogey-6 would have tied for first and sent me into a playoff.

However, in those days they didn't have scoreboards all over the course like you see today. Many of the people around me could have told me that a par would win, and thus relieved me of the need to make a birdie. But I never asked anyone what I needed to win.

Inexperience.

I hit a good drive but it hooked a bit into trampled rough to the left of the fairway. The lie of the ball in the grass was such that I would normally have chosen to swing an iron club.

But the green was 275 yards away. Still thinking I needed a four on the hole, I chose a club that just might give me the distance I thought I needed—the 2-wood. The clubhead barely caught the ball, driving it low and short into a bunker about 160 yards away. It finished in a semi-buried lie.

I'd tried to play a shot that I didn't have the talent to make successfully, at least not very often on the last hole of the U.S. Open.

Inexperience.

I felt I needed to gamble again on my third shot. I thought I needed to reach the green and sink the putt. With the green 110 yards away, and with a five-foot lip on the forward part of the bunker, I tried to clip the ball from the sand with an 8-iron, rather than the sand wedge I would normally have chosen.

The ball flew low—for about four feet. Then it buried in the lip of the bunker.

Again I'd made a bad decision, as it turned out. Again, inexperience.

I finally finished the hole with an eight, two shots behind Byron Nelson, Craig Wood and Denny Shute. Nelson won the playoff.

If there is anything that most older golfers have going for them it is experience. They, more than others, have the background knowledge needed to determine whether or not they can realistically pull off a given shot under a given set of circumstances.

Yet many older players fail to use this experience. They fail to judge their abilities realistically. Too often the older player tries to reach the green with the same club he would have used ten or fifteen years earlier for the distance at hand. That's why you see so many old-timers coming up short of the target.

Too often you see the older players swinging a big, heavy driver off the tee, trying mightily to keep up with the young bucks, when actually they might get more distance—through increased clubhead speed and greater carry through the air—with a 2-wood.

And you see many older, experienced golfers trying to play all but impossible shots from trouble, trying to hook or slice intentionally around a tree, just to gain a few more of those precious yards. In golf, older and bolder is a risky mix.

Older people have more experience not only in golf, but also in life. Yet I see so many of them making the types of wild-hair decisions on the golf course that they would never make away from it. I hate to think of where our country would be if our corporate, political and military people managed their offices as they do their golf games.

Use the experience you have when you play golf. Be objective about your shotmaking decisions. Whenever possible, play the shot you know you can play best. When in doubt, punt.

If you will start to play realistic golf, I think you will find that it is not the ten yards or so you've lost to age that is sending your scores upward. It's probably not even the occasional putt that you miss because of bad nerves. The more likely reason is that you've started to make unrealistic decisions in order to offset these seemingly major, but actually minor, losses to Father Time.

Kiss Yesterday—
and Tomorrow—Goodbye

In 1974, at age 61, I just missed setting a record for being the oldest golfer ever to win a PGA tournament. Dave Stockton edged me by two shots in the Glen Campbell–Los Angeles Open at Riviera Country Club.

In the final round of that event, I was still in contention with only three holes remaining. My mind should have been entirely on my game. However, something was bothering me that I had to square away then and there.

My playing partner was Johnny Miller, and he was struggling with his round. Johnny had won the U.S. Open the year before. Then, about a month ago, he'd won the first three tournaments of l974. But on this particular day he'd seen his chances fade. As a result he had started to play careless golf, hitting his shots with what appeared to be an "I really wish I wasn't here" attitude.

As we walked down the 16th fairway, I finally decided to give this young star some fatherly advice.

"Look, Johnny," I said, "if I didn't like you, I wouldn't say a word, but here you are the Open champion and everybody will be looking at you on TV. And you look like you don't care if you make it through the round.

"They are going to say, 'Look at that snotty-nosed kid. If everything doesn't go to suit him, he doesn't like it.'

"You're only out here four hours," I added. "You should give it your best every minute, whether you're shooting 80 or 60. You just take it from me; try on every shot—I don't care what it is."

On that green he stepped up and knocked in a 20-foot putt. Then he dropped another long one on the last hole.

That night he called me on the telephone.

"Sam," he said, "I want to thank you. I think what you told me did a lot of good. I went from nowhere to fifth place. I won't forget your advice."

Johnny's words, and his nice finish in the tournament, reminded me of another incident that had occurred thirty-six years before. In the 1938 PGA Championship, Jimmy Hines had me on the ropes by the time we reached the 14th green of our match at Shawnee-on-Delaware. I'd just missed a crucial putt. All that Jimmy had to do was drop his 3-footer to win the hole.

However, my missed putt had stopped a few inches from the cup on a direct line between the hole and his ball. In those days we played the stymie rule, so he was not allowed to have me mark my ball and lift it from his path.

All he could do was try to chip his ball over mine and into the hole.

He did just that. His chip shot flew into the cup. That was it, I thought.

But then I noticed that my ball was rolling forward. As his ball had flown through the air, it had barely clipped the top of mine, just enough to start it moving. My ball followed his into the cup.

That freak accident gave me the breathing room I needed. I won the match and went all the way to the finals before losing to Paul Runyan.

The older golfer is supposed to be the wiser golfer. However, true wisdom in golf comes only when you realize how important it is to be patient with yourself when things start going badly.

If you haven't learned that lesson by now, it's time you did. It's time that you realize, and apply, the fact that there is nothing in the world you can do about past bad shots or bad breaks. It doesn't do a bit of good to reflect on what might have been.

You should learn to play golf in the present tense, that being the upcoming shot. Making that shot the best you can is the only thing you can control at the moment.

Walter Hagen won the biggest match-play event of his day, the PGA Championship, five of the seven times he entered it, including four years running, 1924–1927. Against some of the best players in the history of the game, he won thirty-two of thirty-four matches between 1916 and 1927.

Yet Hagen was not as fine a striker of the ball as many of those opponents he defeated. Where he was supreme was in his ability to play in the present tense, to make the shot he needed to make regardless of how badly he'd messed up previous shots.

"I expect to make at least seven mistakes a round," he once said. "Therefore, when I make a bad shot I don't worry about it. It's just one of the seven."

Hagen lived for the moment and played it to the hilt. You should, too. Kiss yesterday goodbye.

And tomorrow too. If it's important to forget about your past mistakes, it's just as important—and perhaps more difficult—to avoid living in the future. Thinking about future holes or shots that you'll be playing, or daydreaming about the great score you'll post if you can just keep it going, can also be dangerous. You see, planning too far ahead also takes your mind away from the present situation. It takes you away from the only shot that you can control at the moment.

How often have you shot one of your best scores ever on the front nine holes and then wasted it all on the back side? How often have you started out with a couple of birdies and then finished with one of your worst scores? Probably your troubles started when you began thinking in the future tense.

When you've got a good round going, you've got to play "cool mad." You've got to work extra hard to concentrate on the shot at hand. If you

don't, you'll tend to get careless and relaxed. That's when the other players start passing you in droves.

When Clayton Heafner, a huge redhead from North Carolina, first joined the PGA tour, he found himself leading the Oakland Open by two shots. In the final round he hit one tee shot deep into the woods and twisted an ankle before he found the ball. His next shot disappeared into a tree and never came out.

Instead of taking an unplayable lie penalty and dropping another ball on safe ground, Heafner climbed the tree, straddled two limbs and made an unbelievable shot. The ball finished just off the green.

From there he chipped the ball to within three inches of the hole. He limped up to where the ball had finished and tapped the 3-incher to the cup. And missed.

After struggling from tee to green, thinking in the present tense all the way, he had let his mind wander from the shot at hand. Jimmy Demaret won the tournament, a single stroke ahead of Heafner.

Before I finish this sermon on never thinking about future holes or past mistakes, I must tell you about the one time I felt a person was truly justified in avoiding the present tense.

It happened many years ago at the Greenbrier. I was about to give a very prim and proper woman a few pointers before she started her round. She was obviously a bit self-conscious, standing in front of the people gathered around the tee, so I suggested she take a few practice swings to loosen up.

This she did. After a few swings, however, I noticed a pink object that was starting to work its way out of the V-neck of her blouse.

Before I could say anything, she made another swing. Out popped one of her falsies. It bounced on the ground in front of her, rolled around in a couple of circles and then settled to a stop, pointing upward.

There was this awful silence. Someone had to say something to break the tension.

"That's OK," I finally volunteered. "Just leave it there and we'll use it as a tee."

She dashed to the clubhouse, lopsided and sobbing. I never saw her again.

There are times when even the best of us cannot bear to play in the present tense.

Getting More
from Your Body

I had won my third Miami Open in 1950, playing the back nine at Miami Springs Country Club in thirty shots. The next year I took this title for the fourth time.

It was now 1955, however, and I was still looking for my fifth victory in this event. In the final round, playing in 100-degree weather, I had shot a less-than-startling 35 on the front nine. Once again it looked like I was out of the running.

Then suddenly my game turned hotter than the weather. I finished the round in 64, with a record-setting 29 over the final nine holes. Just maybe it would take the prize.

I was sitting in a car with a friend, waiting to see if my score would hold up. He was drinking beer from a cup at the time. My throat was parched. The temptation was overwhelming.

"Gee," I said to him, "I sure could go for a sip of that beer."

Now, I've never been a drinker—never been drunk in my life. A glass of beer or a sweet daiquiri is just about my limit. But I took a couple of gulps of my friend's beer—no more. Then I learned that Tommy Bolt had tied me for first place. There would be a sudden-death playoff.

As I walked to the first tee, that beer I'd just swallowed hit me like a right cross to the jaw. I felt absolutely woozy.

I swung at my tee shot feeling like I was floating in space. The ball flew far to the right of the fairway, heading for sure into a group of

trees. Somehow, miraculously, it finished in a clearing where I could at least make a full swing on my next shot.

I chose a 2-iron, and sliced that shot intentionally around some more trees. It finished on the green about fifty feet from the hole.

Meanwhile Bolt's drive had come to rest in the fairway, but just in front of an anthill. Unable to obtain relief from the poor lie, he pushed his second shot—a 4-wood—to the right of the green. After he chipped badly on his third shot, Tommy was fuming as only he could fume.

"Did someone kick your ball out of those trees," he asked as we prepared to putt.

I just smiled and said,"You gonna play at Sanford next week?"

I two-putted for my par. Tommy missed his try. I'd finally won my fifth Miami Open.

I'd also learned a lesson. Never again would I drink anything stronger than soda pop during competition.

Living in moderation has paid full dividends for me over the years; I'm sure of that. I've not only stayed away from the hooch, but I've also refrained from smoking, at least since way back when I was starting high school. I did take a couple of puffs many years ago when I was doing some cigarette commercials but my mouth tasted terrible for a week.

Maybe I won't convince you to give up drinking and smoking in order to play better golf longer—that's your business—but I do feel obligated to point out that both can affect your skills. Alcohol, like caffeine, can make you jumpy under pressure, and older people especially don't need something extra to stimulate those frayed nerves.

Smoking can be relaxing, I'm sure, but I don't think most smokers would need that crutch in the first place if they could kick the habit. If you find yourself short of breath and weak in the legs after climbing a hill on your course, you would be wise to try abstaining for at least a week or so. I'll bet even money that those hills would seem shorter—and your succeeding shots would be longer—if you could pass that one-week hurdle.

I'll be talking about all the things that a fat stomach can do to ruin your golf swing in a later chapter (see "Golf Magic—Turning Pounds into Yards"), and I've said enough about drinking and smoking. However, I do have some other thoughts on how the older golfer can improve his or her game by taking a little better care of himself, or herself, both off and on the course.

Off the course I recommend exercises that will accomplish the following:

1. Strengthen your legs. When you lose your wheels, you can forget about playing good golf. Skipping rope, jogging or even just running in place will work wonders in no time. They will also improve your lung capacity. In golf you need plenty of oxygen, especially late in the round and when you're under pressure. I advise against playing tennis, however; it trains your muscles to make a swing that is detrimental to hitting a golf ball well.

2. Strengthen your abdominal muscles. Older players, especially, need a firm midsection in order to make a full turn back and through, and to swing the club on a proper plane.

3. Improve your flexibility. To do this I know of nothing better than simply swinging a weighted club back and forth whenever you feel the urge, hopefully at least three or four times a week. If you can't find such a club to buy, just wrap some lead tape around the head of an old wood club. This will both stretch and strengthen all of your golfing muscles.

On the course I recommend that you:

1. Wrap your arms around a club that you've placed across your back. Then make a few turns back and through. Do this whenever you feel tight before or during a round.

2. Take a deep breath, in and out, before you swing or putt.

3. Walk rather than ride if at all possible. If your club's rules force you to take a cart, let your riding partner do the driving while you walk at least some of the holes.

4. On those hot, sunny days be sure to wear a hat. Also, use your umbrella for cooling protection. Seek out the shade when you walk

down the fairway and await your turn to shoot. Wrap a cool wet towel around the back of your neck and remoisten it when you can. Drink plenty of water during the round. Carry salt tablets in your bag and take one between nines.

5. Carry a bottle of glucose or honey in your bag. A sip or two along the way is the best remedy I know of for overcoming late-round fatigue.

6. Eat only light foods, sparingly, before or during your round.

Older but Wiser—
Learn Your Rights

I've had my share of frustrations in golf, but one instance in Chicago still stands out in my mind.

It seemed like everything was going against me that day. One bad thing led to another until I finally found myself looking at two golf balls, each partially buried beyond identification, in a river bed.

I knew that one of the balls was mine, but I didn't know which it was. And at that point I didn't much care either.

I did know that the rules said I couldn't touch my ball because it was in a hazard. All I could do was choose between the two balls and blast it out. Then, if it wasn't mine, I could go back and play the other ball without penalty.

I chose the ball that looked easier to play and gave it a chop. It flew out free and clear, but straight into more mud on the opposite bank. Splat.

Now I was really hot. I charged up to the ball and gave it another whack. My clubhead slammed into the mud, where it stuck. Splat again.

I looked up to watch the ball in flight. It was nowhere to be seen.

Now I was really in a fix. It looked like I'd lost a ball that I didn't even know for sure was mine.

But it wasn't lost after all. As I lifted my clubhead from the mud the ball came with it, pasted against the clubface with nature's own glue.

I'd found the ball—and it was mine—but now I faced another predicament: how could I hit it when it was already stuck to my club.

I asked Ray Mangrum, my playing partner, what I should do.

"Looks to me like you didn't finish your swing, Sam. Why don't you make a follow-through? Maybe the ball will come unstuck."

I thought Ray's idea was a good one, but wondered if maybe I could gain a little advantage.

"What if I walked up to the green and just sort of flipped it into the hole?" I asked.

Ray didn't think that would be fair.

I really didn't know my rights, but I did take Ray's suggestion about finishing my swing. I gave the club a nice swish forward and, sure enough, the ball flew off the clubface, safely out of the hazard.

Naturally there was a devil of a discussion back at the clubhouse after my round, but the tournament officials seemed to think I'd done the right thing.

I wasn't sure if I had or not, but I did know that I'd made one of the slowest forward swings in the history of golf. It must have taken at least two, maybe three, minutes between starting my downswing and finishing my follow-through.

Looking back on that incident, I figure I was lucky that the officials didn't penalize me, or maybe disqualify me altogether. Since then it has been ruled that in cases where the ball sticks to the clubface you count the stroke you've made, pick the ball off the club, drop it over your shoulder at the original position and continue play without penalty.

It really pays to become familiar with the rules. Older people are supposed to be wiser; right? Well, maybe a little rules knowledge will help make up for some of the distance you might be losing off the tee.

The rules exist not only to explain your *duties* as a golfer, but also your *rights*. There are many times when these rights can actually help you shoot a lower score, or beat an opponent.

For instance, there's the matter of "relief." You are allowed relief, without penalty, from certain things that might adversely affect your stance, your swing or the lie of your ball. You are allowed relief from "ground under repair," "materials piled for removal," a temporary accumulation of water, an "immovable obstruction," or a cast, hole or runway made by a burrowing animal, reptile or bird.

If you come up against one of these situations when your ball is in a fairway or even in the rough, you have the right to first find the nearest spot of relief that is not nearer the hole. You then pick up your ball, face the hole and drop the ball over your shoulder so that it touches down within two club-lengths of that spot. Use your longest club for measuring.

Now, what many golfers don't realize is that the rules allow that ball to bounce and roll ANOTHER two club-lengths from where it touches down. Thus it is possible for your ball to finish up to four club-lengths from the spot of relief.

Also, the rules don't differentiate between rough and fairway—it's all considered "through the green." Therefore, many times you can drop on a spot that causes your ball to roll out of the rough and into the fairway, or out from behind a tree or a bush.

It's all legal so long as (1) your ball doesn't finally finish nearer the hole than the original position from where you lifted it, (2) it doesn't hit you or your clothing before touching the ground as you drop it, (3) it doesn't roll into a sand or water hazard or out of bounds, or (4) it doesn't finish more than two club-lengths from where it touched down when you dropped it.

If any of these four things happen, then you must redrop, but without penalty. But that can also be to your advantage, especially if you didn't particularly like the lie you received on the first drop. Whenever you get a bad drop, be sure to check to see if the drop fit all four of those requirements. If it didn't—if, say, the ball rolled into a pond or a sand trap—then you can redrop.

If your second drop also doesn't fit all requirements, then you are allowed to place the ball in proper position. You don't see many folks placing their ball in a bad lie.

You might also be interested to know that you can stand out of bounds to hit a ball that is still in bounds, or that you can have someone stand at the hole and hold the flagstick over their head, so you can see it from down in the boondocks.

Now, here's a good thing to know about the rules governing head-to-head match play, the competition used in most club championships: Let's say your opponent putts his ball and it finishes near the hole. He steps up and putts again, knocking the ball into the hole. Or, he refrains from putting out, but marks and lifts his ball instead.

In either case he has probably overstepped his rights.

He does not have the right to putt out if his ball is closer to the hole than yours. You are "away" and have the right to putt first. You may ask him either to replace his ball, or to replace it and then mark and lift it.

This can all prove embarrassing and disconcerting to your opponent. However, he's the one who didn't follow the rules; not you.

Moreover, there will be times when you will want your opponent's ball on the green, rather than marked and lifted or holed out. For instance, if his ball is behind the hole from yours, it might backstop yours from running too far beyond. Or, if his ball is alongside the hole, it might allow your ball to carom off his and into the cup. If your ball should strike your opponent's, you do not suffer a penalty.

Beware, however, that he does have the right either to replace his ball where it originally lay, or to play from where it finishes after being struck by yours. If your ball should happen to knock your foe's into the hole, he will have finished the hole with his previous stroke.

In short, in match-play competition between two individuals—but not in stroke play or four-ball team matches—the person whose ball is away has the right to determine whether or not his opponent may or may not mark his or her ball.

You might also be interested in knowing that the rules do not prohibit you from practicing on the course before a match—so long as the local rules do not say otherwise. A few putts on a nearby green before teeing off is a nice way to build a realistic feel for the speed of the

greens you'll play that day. Don't try it before a stroke-play event, however. You'll be disqualified.

I don't know anyone who has all the answers for every possible rules situation that might come up in golf. The "Rules of Golf" do, however, give you clear-cut ground rules for making a fair and correct judgment. They are available in booklet form—handy for carrying in your golf bag—from the United States Golf Association, Far Hills, New Jersey 07931, for fifty cents.

I'll warn you now that the rules demand careful reading. Every word seems to have a specific purpose and therefore must be taken literally. (If the book says you can drop away from a hole made by a "burrowing animal, reptile or bird," it means just that. Dropping away from an anthill would be illegal.)

However, close study of the rules will not only prove rewarding in terms of helping your scoring and increasing your status around the club; it will also give you a much deeper understanding and appreciation of the game.

Improving Your Long Game

Your First Priority— A Good Grip

I'd like to tell you about a retired lawyer down in Florida because he's typical of many older golfers I've taught and played with; he'd like to hit the ball a little bit farther.

"I can't reach some of these par-4 holes in two shots," he told me one day at the Pine Tree Golf Club in Delray Beach.

I worked with him a bit and found that there were two main reasons why his shots were so short.

First, they were not going high enough in the air.

"You don't get the ball carrying far enough," I pointed out. "It hits the ground too soon. Then it doesn't run too far because these fairways are so well watered and fairly soft."

The second reason his shots were so short was that he couldn't give the club much zip into the ball. His wrists were too stiff.

I explained to the man that both reasons for his lack of distance lay mainly in the way he held the club with his right hand. He was clenching it too much in the palm instead of the fingers.

I told him that this grip was making his swing very flat. His hands weren't even coming up to his shoulders at the top of the backswing.

"That makes it tough to get the ball up high," I explained, "especially with the driver. We'll change your grip a little bit and you'll start swinging more upright. Then your ball will come off the ground a little higher and carry farther. You'll be able to reach those greens."

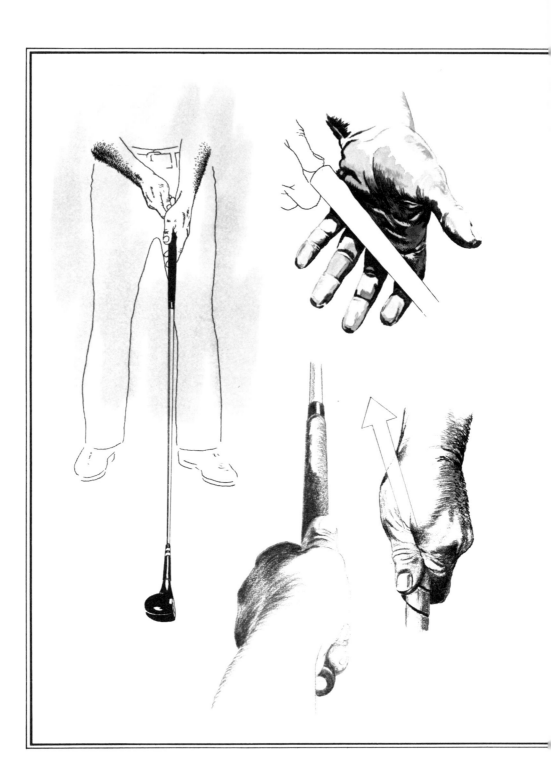

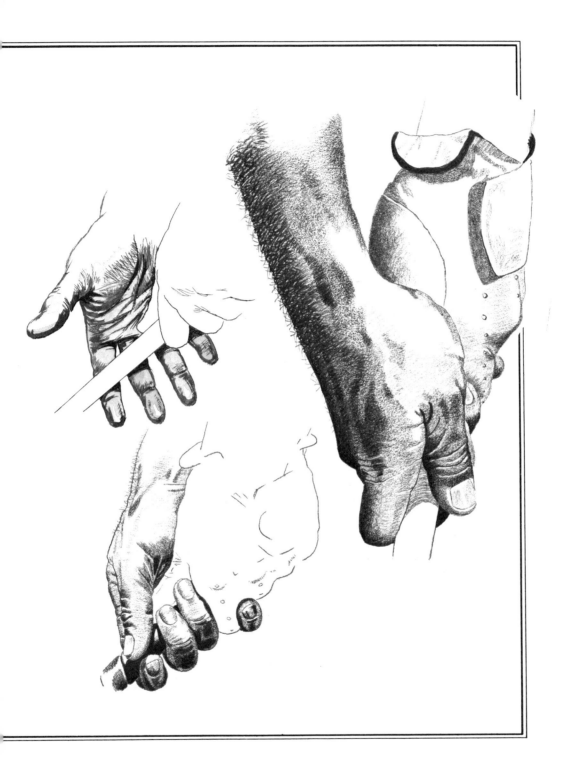

I showed him how to hold the club more in the fingers of his right hand, but he didn't like the way it felt.

"That feels weak, Sam. I feel as if I don't have any control of the club."

With that I took a golf ball and placed it in the palm of his right hand. I closed all his fingers around it so he was clenching the ball like he'd been clenching the club.

"How far do you think you could throw this ball?" I asked.

"I couldn't throw it anywhere," he admitted.

Then I asked him to hold the ball with just the ends of his thumb and first two fingers.

"Now could you wing it?" I asked.

"Sure could," he said.

I thought I'd made a believer out of my pupil. I was sure of it when he mentioned that his friend, Lou Graham, the 1975 U.S. Open champion, had given him the same advice.

But I was wrong. The man hit some really nice shots with his new grip, but only when he tried it out on the practice tee. On the course, with a few dollars on the line, he still goes back to his old grip. It feels safer, more comfortable. He still comes up short on those par-4 holes. I guess he always will.

I'm as sure as a toad is ugly that the No. 1 problem of older golfers is a bad grip. I'd say that 98 percent of the over-forty golfers I've seen need to improve their hold on the club. Even a slight change would help their scores.

Actually, almost all golfers have a bad grip. It's just that most older players have had a longer time to make it feel comfortable. And they seem reluctant to make a change after so many years. Some do try, but then they miss a shot or two so they revert back to habit.

I can't go along with this attitude. If I'd tried something for thirty or forty years and it hadn't worked too well, I'd sure figure it was about time to change.

The older golfer, especially, needs a good grip. When you start losing some of your youthful flexibility and precise hand-eye coordination, you need to put your hands in a position that really lets you bust that ball with as free a swing as you can muster. A bad grip makes you compensate somewhere during the stroke, and compensations usually inhibit freedom of movement. That means less distance and, possibly, less accuracy than you deserve.

We've got some drawings here showing how I position my hands on the club. My grip is pretty standard, and I think it's a darn good model for you to copy. Here are the things I think you should notice in particular:

1. Be sure you assume your grip with the club soled flat on the ground and more or less straight out from just inside your left heel. The shaft should extend upward toward the inside of your left thigh.

2. Rest your left hand along the target side of the shaft. The shaft should run diagonally across the palm, extending upward from the top section of the forefinger to just under the butt or heel pad of the palm.

3. When you close your fingers and palm around the club, your thumb should ride comfortably down and across the shaft to the top-right side as you look down on it. The "V" formed between this thumb and your forefinger should point toward your right shoulder.

4. With your right hand you should hold the club more in your fingers and not so much in the palm. When you close this hand, its little finger should either lap over or interlock with the forefinger of the left. Your right thumb pad should snuggle against your left thumb.

5. You should "trigger" the club with your right thumb and forefinger, just as if you're shooting a pistol. This will cause a little bit of spacing between your forefinger and middle finger.

6. When your grip is completed, the "V" between your right thumb and forefinger should also point toward your right shoulder.

At first this may sound like a complicated procedure, but stick with it until your finished grip looks like mine. You might check it in a mirror.

If this positioning of the hands is different from what you've been using, it will feel uncomfortable at first. The more you use it, however, the more natural it will seem. In time your old grip will feel unnatural.

I urge you to start getting familiar with this grip by practicing your short shots from around the practice green. Then gradually work into full swings—first with the shorter iron clubs—on the practice tee.

Don't be surprised if you hit some bad shots at first. This will happen because you've been making compensations in your swing to offset the bad grip. Your shots will improve eventually and become better than ever once your nerves and muscles sense that now, with the proper grip, these unnecessary complications are no longer needed.

Be patient and give the new grip a chance. Work with it. I can't think of a better way for any golfer to spend his or her practice time.

Finally, in the next piece of instruction in this book, I'll be talking about grip pressure. This is something you should learn to apply correctly to get full benefit from the proper grip position I've just described.

Grip Pressure—
Light Is Right

One of my good friends is Bob Toski, who was leading moneywinner on the pro tour in 1954. I call him "Mouse" because he stands about 5 feet 7 inches and weighs only 127 pounds. We used to say he was the only man around who needed a lifeguard to take a shower.

But pound for pound, Toski, who is now fifty, still hits a golf ball farther than any man I've ever seen. He's also a giant when it comes to teaching the game.

Bob's main message for his pupils is a light grip pressure, both before and throughout the stroke. I'm sure that his own light grip accounts in large part for his unusually long and accurate shots.

One day Bob was teaching a fellow who looked like he was trying to manhandle the golf club. He had a real white-knuckle grip. As a result, he couldn't hit the ball much past his shadow.

Finally Bob asked his pupil how he would like to be operated on by a surgeon who gripped the scalpel as tightly as he was holding the golf club.

With that the man burst out laughing.

"What's so funny?" Toski asked.

"I AM a surgeon," the man replied.

Needless to say, Bob's student got the message. His shots immediately began flying farther and straighter.

I was like Bob's pupil when I started at golf as a youngster back

home in Virginia. I'd been playing a lot of baseball where I held the bat like I was trying to squeeze it into sawdust. Naturally I applied the same grip pressure to golf, trying to give the ball a home-run wallop down in the pasture of my folks' cow and chicken farm.

It took a lot of experimenting, but I finally figured out that all this grip pressure was freezing my arms and wrists. I found I could hit the ball farther when I held the club lightly, like I did when I was pitching a baseball.

Later I had the opportunity to teach golf to Gene Tunney, the former world heavyweight boxing champion. Tunney looked like a man who should hit the ball 400 yards, but at first he couldn't move it half that far. He was trying to give every shot a knockout punch, but all that extra tension was making him swing like a robot. He had all the strength in the world, but it was stifling his clubhead speed.

The message here is that hitting golf balls far and straight is more a matter of speed and flexibility than brute strength. It's a message that applies to everyone, but especially to the older player.

As we grow older, our muscles tend to lose their flexibility. Backswings get shorter. Arm speed into the ball slows down. Shots don't go as far as they once did.

For many older players, the natural reaction is to fight back by swinging harder. As a result they unconsciously grip the club tighter and tighter.

Nothing could be more self-defeating. This extra grip pressure creates even more wrist and arm tension. This tension makes backswings still shorter and clubhead speed even slower. Shots get shorter and shorter; grip pressure gets tighter and tighter.

The way to break this vicious cycle is to practice what Toski—and Snead—preach. Consciously hold the club as lightly—but not loosely—as you can. Imagine that you're holding a small, fragile chicken with just enough pressure to keep it from escaping.

Try it. With this light grip pressure, swing a club back and forth, slowly at first and then faster and faster. Gradually increase the speed of your motion, but NOT the pressure of your grip.

Keep swinging faster until it feels like the club is about to fly from your hands. At that point merely increase slightly the amount of pressure you are applying with the last two fingers of your left hand. Hold on with just enough firmness in these fingers to keep the club from slipping.

As you swing the club back and forth, you should try to sense a lightness in your arms, a dramatic freedom from tension.

Also, your wrists should feel oily. They should cock and uncock NATURALLY, merely as a RESULT of your arms swinging and the club moving. Don't try to make them uncock, because that will make you increase your right-hand grip pressure.

The point of this drill is to show you just how lightly you can hold the club THROUGHOUT your swing, and how fast your arms can swing the club when they are free of tension. It is this speed of movement that will restore your distance and, perhaps, even give you some *extra* length.

When you actually start to hit some shots, your natural tendency will be to hold the club tighter from the start, or to grab or throw it during your swing. You must resist this temptation.

Start by hitting practice shots with the ball teed. Just hold the club lightly as you swing it through the ball. Learn to trust the feeling of lightness in your hands and arms, and the oiliness in your wrists. Then, finally, take that same feeling into shots from the grass.

For most players, learning to trust a lighter grip pressure will take quite a bit of conscious effort. Once you build this trust, however, you will be amazed at how fast and far that ball jumps off your clubface. It will all seem so effortless.

Pull the
Trigger Sooner

By 1942 I'd won twenty-five tournaments on the pro circuit in less than six years. I'd been leading moneywinner in 1938, and second or third each of the other years.

However, some people were still wondering if I had enough courage to win one of our three major championships—the PGA, the U.S. Open or the Masters. Twice I'd finished second in PGA. I'd been runner-up once in each of the others.

The 1942 PGA Championship looked like my last chance to prove myself for some time. The war was threatening to close down many tournaments, and I was on the verge of enlisting in the Navy. In fact, I'd actually delayed my enlistment briefly so that I could first compete in the PGA at the Seaview Country Club, Atlantic City, New Jersey.

There I advanced to the finals by beating Sam Byrd, Willie Goggin, Ed Dudley and Jimmy Demaret. My final foe was to be Corporal Jim Turnesa, a solid competitor from a large family of outstanding golfers. Turnesa's early-round victims had included Dutch Harrison, Jug Mc-Spaden, Ben Hogan and Byron Nelson. Obviously the young corporal could play.

And play he did. Spurred on by a loud, one-sided gallery that seemed to include every soldier from nearby Ft. Dix, Corporal Turnesa seemed likely to drown this would-be sailor. After we'd played twenty-three holes of the scheduled thirty-six, he had me three down.

Turnesa did, occasionally, mis-hit a shot. Each time, however, he recovered magnificently. He simply stepped up to the next shot, waggled the clubhead a couple of times—his standard pre-shot routine—and slapped the ball in close enough to the flagstick to halve the hole.

Starting with the 24th hole, I began putting more and more pressure on Turnesa. I started covering the flagstick with my approach shots. My birdie putts started dropping. I did win a couple of holes, but Turnesa continued to play his own steady game, seemingly unconcerned about his dwindling lead.

I kept looking for a sign that he might be cracking. I needed some assurance to keep my own nerves in tow. Nothing.

Even after I tied the match on the 27th hole, where he missed a 3-foot putt, the young soldier seemed calm and collected, ready to fight me down to the final green and, if necessary, beyond.

I drove on the 28th tee and stood by as Turnesa set up to his shot. Then it hit me. Something was wrong. Something was different.

My eye saw it, but my brain didn't figure it out, at least not until Turnesa's drive had flown into the woods down the left side of the fairway. Then it registered.

Turnesa had not prepared for the shot in his normal fashion. Instead of waggling the clubhead twice, he had moved it back and forth at least four times. And the movements had been deliberate and jerky, not smooth and flowing.

At that moment I knew I was on top of the match, that I had Turnesa on the ropes. My own confidence soared; my nervousness disappeared completely. I did, in fact, win the match—and my first major title—going away.

The tip-off, of course, had been the extra waggles. What they told me was simply that Turnesa had lost his confidence. For twenty-seven holes he had played decisive, forthright golf. The extra waggles—a subtle variation from his normal pre-shot routine—suggested that he had started to second-guess himself. He needed the extra waggles to give himself time to make up his mind. It was that extra time over the ball that, in the end, upset his swing tempo and caused him to pull the drive into the trees.

I find that many older golfers spend too much time over the ball before they start the swing. The longer you stand at the address position, the easier it is for those older muscles and ligaments to get all stoved up. That's the surest way I know to force yourself into making a quick, short and jerky swing.

The older golfer, especially, needs to reduce tension—both mental and physical—by pulling the trigger sooner, once he's set up to the shot. The late Bobby Jones had one of the smoothest swings in the history of the game and, not coincidentally, one of the shortest pre-swing routines imaginable: right foot set, left foot set, backswing started. Julius Boros is another who almost seems to walk into his swing. It's as smooth as STP.

It will take some practice for most golfers to shorten the time they spend addressing the ball. It will also take some mental discipline to force yourself to do it on the course.

Mostly, however, you will need to do a much more thorough job of settling things in your mind—what shot to play; which club to use; how to swing—BEFORE you set up to the ball.

If you should run into some doubt once you're over the ball, then back away and start over. Free up your mind and your body about what you intend to do. Then set up once again and fire away.

I think you will find that shortening your time over the ball before swinging will improve your shots on two accounts. First, you'll swing with greater freedom and better rhythm because of reduced muscle tension. Second, your whole approach to your shots will be more positive. You'll have eliminated all that time over the ball that you once gave to thinking about how you might miss it.

Press Forward
Before Starting Back

I'll never forget this older man who came to me for golf lessons several years ago. I'd guess that he was well into his sixties at the time.

Before our first lesson, the man told me why he'd decided to improve his game. He explained that he had developed a very close relationship with this much younger woman, who also was extremely athletic. Specifically, he hoped that I could increase the length of his golf shots so that he could at least keep up with his girl friend.

I certainly admired and understood the man's reason for taking lessons. After my first look at his golf swing, however, I wished he'd never met the young lady.

It was painfully obvious that my pupil badly lacked coordination—at least for golf. His backswing was little more than a lifting of the club with his hands and arms as his weight shifted FORWARD, toward the target. His forward swing was a chopping action, well suited for splitting timber, with his weight shifting BACKWARD onto his right foot.

Somehow I had to find a way to make this man completely reverse the directions in which he was shifting his weight.

Both teacher and pupil flunked that first lesson. The more things I suggested to make him shift his weight back and then forward, rather than forward and then back, the more he started turning into a human pretzel. Finally, I suggested that he rest his body and his mind, and return the next day for a fresh try.

That evening I was walking back to my car. I happened to look over toward the tennis courts. There I saw my pupil and his girl friend having a friendly match.

I was some distance away, and he was involved in the match, so I didn't interrupt their play. But I did watch my man play a few points. I couldn't believe what I saw.

He played tennis with the rhythm and grace of a superb athlete. He looked half his age as he moved around the court.

I was especially interested in his serve, a long, flowing motion that rifled the ball across the net. At that moment I knew I'd found my key for improving his golf swing.

The next day I told my pupil how impressed I'd been with his skill at tennis. Then I began relating that ability to his golf swing. First I handed him a golf ball.

"I'd like you to show me how you'd serve this golf ball, if you had a tennis racket in your hand."

He took the ball in his left hand. Then he leaned forward toward an imaginary target, his weight shifting onto his left foot. It was a slight movement, hardly noticeable, but it was definitely a forward pressing of weight onto his left foot.

Then, in direct reaction to that forward press, he went immediately into his backswing, his toss of the ball, and finally his forward stroke. His weight shifted to his right foot going back and then forward again onto his left.

The man could shift his weight perfectly when serving a tennis ball, primarily because he included the forward press onto his left foot before he began to swing his arm and shift his weight back to his right side.

In just a matter of minutes I had my pupil making a similar forward press in his golf swing. The initial movement to the left forced him to shift weight onto his right foot during his backswing, which made him shift back to the left on his forward swing.

Once he began shifting his weight back and forward in the same direction he was swinging the club, his legs and his whole body started contributing to his stroke. It became more than a mere chopping action with his arms. Naturally, he started getting the extra distance he'd been looking for.

Golf is the toughest game in the world to play well. One reason is that you have to start the action. No one is pitching the ball toward you, or hitting it in your direction with a racket or paddle. There is nothing to react to as in tennis or baseball or Ping-Pong; nothing to make your nerves and muscles work smoothly and naturally.

Instead that ball is just sitting there. It's up to you to make everything begin to move correctly. Too often we start with a lift or a jerk, rather than a nice slow, smooth, coordinated motion.

It's the forward press that helps overcome our inertia. It's nothing more than a slight movement to the left. Both hands gently press the top of the club very slightly forward toward the target as the right knee inclines toward the ball. Then the backswing begins immediately as a reflex or rebound action out of the forward press.

The forward press makes the swing itself begin as a coordinated movement with the club and our arms, body and legs all working together as a unit. It also makes them work at a smoother and, usually, a slower pace.

I've never had a pupil who didn't play golf better after he or she learned to make a forward press. It's especially necessary, however, for older golfers who often need more distance on their shots. They need a way to make all parts of the anatomy do their fair share in producing clubhead speed. They also need to coordinate these parts with a swing that is rhythmical and smoothly paced. The forward press helps put everything together.

14

More Length
with Less Effort

It was one of those nice moments in the life of a professional golfer. Barring heart attack, heat prostration or an earthquake, I knew that I was going to be the 1936 West Virginia PGA champion.

As I stood on the 18th tee of the Greenbrier course in White Sulphur Springs with the tournament in my pocket, all I wanted was a drive that finished somewhere in the fairway. I really didn't care about hitting it far. A nice soft, safe tee shot would do just fine.

I still remember how I held the club very gently in my hands. My backswing was slow and easy. My forward swing seemed effortless.

But the ball exploded off the clubface. It took off and flew—on and on and on. I couldn't believe the length it carried. And I'd swung so easily.

I finally birdied the hole—for a 61.

Since that day over forty years ago, I've played that same golf course at least a thousand times. Never have I driven the ball so far on that particular hole.

I had a similar experience a few years later in Selma, Alabama, during an exhibition match. The course we were playing had this one hole that was 295 yards long. All the local folks wondered if Snead could drive the green.

On the tee, the man in charge of the gallery announced that I would

hit two drives on this hole. He explained that the first would be my regular shot. The second would be my try to reach the green.

Naturally, my goal on the first drive was merely to get my ball in position for an easy approach shot to the green and a possible birdie—so I had no intention of giving it full effort. I was saving the muscle for my second drive.

Once again I swung the club back slowly and then forward effortlessly. Again the ball exploded off the clubface. It finished some fifteen yards BEYOND the green.

"Looks like I'll need that second shot for chipping back," I said to the marshal.

I hope that these two examples help make clear this point: You will hit the ball farther more frequently when you don't try to hit it far.

Perhaps you've had similar experiences. Or perhaps you've had times when you've tried to hit a fairway wood from a fairly tight lie. The ball's sitting down low in the grass and all you've tried to do is simply make solid contact—and the shot's gone farther than you ever thought it would.

Or perhaps you make better contact on shots that are downwind than you do when pressing for distance against a strong breeze.

Or maybe you hit better shots from an elevated tee when the fairway slopes downward, rather than upward, in front of you.

All these situations tend to prove that same point. Again, we tend to get more length when our mind is less concerned about knocking out a home run.

I find that older golfers are especially vulnerable when it comes to pressing for distance. One day they find that their shots aren't going quite so far. Then they start trying to regain this lost yardage by swinging harder. That's when the real loss of distance starts to set in.

I normally hit my shots—even my drives—with about 85 percent effort. I might reach back for an extra ten or fifteen yards on an open par-5 hole, if it looks like I might reach the green in two shots rather than three. But that's a rare occasion. If I tried for those extra few yards every time, I'd be shooting in the 80s, and spending a lot more time fishing and hunting.

Now, I know a lot of people who read this book will be looking for more distance. I know it's an especially big concern for older players. So I'm not going to duck the issue.

What I do want you to understand, however, is that all my advice on adding length will be wasted if you are swinging the club—and yourself—faster than you can control.

This is especially true on drives. We get that No. 1 wood in our hands and it's Katie bar the door. Subconsciously we seem to sense that this club is built for distance. We hold on to it a bit tighter than we should. The tension creeps up our arms and into our shoulders. It makes us swing shorter and faster with a club that should be swung longer and slower.

I've seen countless golfers—especially women and older men—actually add distance merely by choking down an inch or two on their woods and longer iron clubs.

I've seen others increase their length by holding the club lighter than seems normal, so long as they keep their grip light all the way through impact and beyond.

Others add considerable length simply by thinking about swinging THROUGH the ball, not just TO it.

And I've certainly seen players hit it farther when they started using only 85 percent effort.

Remember that distance comes not only from clubhead speed, but also from solid contact. All the clubhead speed in the world isn't going to mean much if it doesn't even scare the ball.

Cut back your effort 15 percent. You just might find your shots going 15 percent farther.

15

Use Your Feet for Extra Yards

I guess every golf instructor has had at least one student he wished had never put on spikes.

For me it was a man who actually flew his divots farther than he did the ball.

This man came to me for a lesson and started hitting some shots with the fastest, jerkiest, least rhythmical swing I'd ever seen. He had sod flying so fast and furious I felt like I was in the middle of World War II.

After a few minutes this human plow was gasping and panting, and making my lesson tee look like sowing time in the Corn Belt.

Somehow I had to stop this mutilation. I had to come up with something that would slow him down and put a little rhythm into his stroke.

"You know," I finally said, "a lot of the old-time players used to swing in waltz time—tra-la-la-la BOOM tra-la, tra-la . . . ; tra-la-la-la BOOM tra-la, tra-la . . ."

My man looked at me and smiled.

"I should know something about that," he said. "I'm a professional dancer."

I told him to stop jitterbugging and start waltzing.

He did, and I've never seen anyone improve so much, so fast, in my whole life. In just seconds he went from idiot to scholar, from zero right up the ladder.

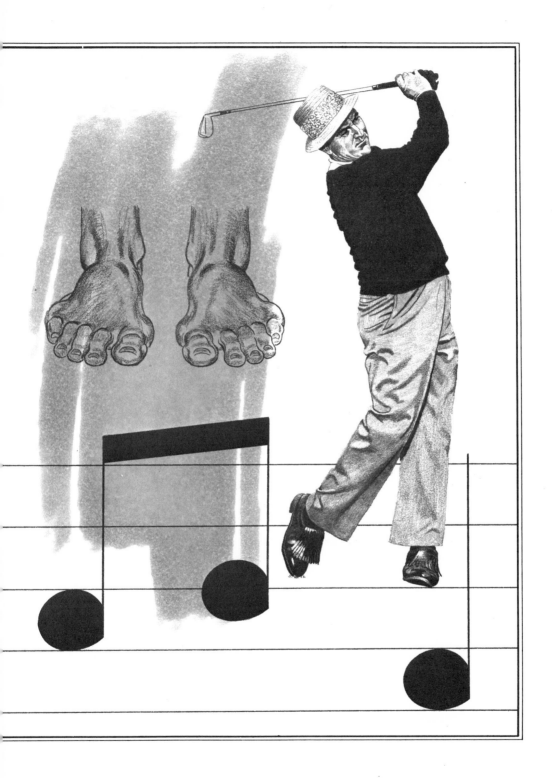

I don't expect all readers to turn their games around like that man did; obviously we aren't all expert dancers. But there are other ways to improve the rhythm of your golf swing.

Good rhythm is most important for older players because it translates into extra distance. It gets the various parts of the anatomy moving at the right time, so that the clubhead moves faster into the ball.

Good rhythm also helps make that clubhead move on the right path, and face in the right direction, so all that extra clubhead speed gets squarely applied to the ball.

The problem with us old-timers is that when we try to get more distance we automatically start using the parts that ruin, instead of help, our rhythm. We instinctively start working our hands and wrists to make the clubhead go faster. Or we start laboring our shoulders, because we've used them throughout our lives when we wanted to apply some strength. Laboring the shoulders reduces distance. It makes the arms—and the club itself—swing slower, and off-path.

The last things that most golfers use for extra distance are really the first things they should accentuate: their feet. This is true largely because it is good footwork that produces good rhythm. That's why my dancer-pupil did so well; as soon as I mentioned waltz time, he instinctively related to his feet. As his footwork improved, so did his shots.

When I was a youngster I learned to play golf barefooted. No one told me to do it that way, but that's how I lived, from the last frost in the spring until the first of winter. Shoes were for church and, later, social occasions.

I'm convinced that learning golf in bare feet had a great deal to do with my developing a rhythmical swing. I know that the game started getting more difficult when I got older and had to start wearing shoes.

I remember one time when a bunch of writers were asking me about playing barefooted. I was at Augusta National at the time, warming up for the Masters. I shucked off my shoes and played my round barefooted—birdied the first two holes and shot 68.

Over the years I've always found that practicing barefooted was a sure way to get my rhythm and balance back in tune.

What happens when you swing without shoes on is that you'll lose your balance if you don't swing rhythmically. Start laboring your shoulders or swinging too fast and, without the support of your shoes, you'll feel like falling down.

Your body senses this will happen, so you start swinging rhythmically—automatically.

If you don't feel like practicing barefooted, just hit some shots with your feet together. The same thing happens; you unconsciously sense that you'd better swing rhythmically or you'll end up on your bottom. Most people are amazed at how well they can hit shots this way. But be sure you put your feet smack-dab together. You might miss the first few shots, but stick with it. In a short time you'll start feeling what a rhythmical swing really is.

On the course during play you might not wish to hit shots with your feet together. Then, when your rhythm is off, just put them together as you make a few practice swings before your next shot. Again, try to feel the pace and rhythm of your swing as you do. Then merely duplicate that feeling on your actual shot.

Good footwork makes your legs and hips join in with the rest of your anatomy. Thus it adds a few more parts to the whole. When you've got these parts contributing, you'll be less likely to rely subconsciously on your hands and shoulders, which, again, are the parts that tend to ruin your rhythm.

To get good footwork I've always tried to work on the insides of my feet. On full shots I set up to the ball with more weight on the inside of my right foot than anywhere else. Then, during my backswing, my right leg becomes sort of an axis, around which my body turns and my arms swing the club.

I roll onto the inside of my left foot during my backswing as my left knee swings to the right. I'd never get onto the inside of the foot—and I'd never make a full turn—if my knee kicked straight forward instead of to the right.

One of the best golfers of all time was Horton Smith. I played many rounds with him in the 1930s and '40s, and I got so I could almost always tell when he was going to make a bad shot. It didn't happen too often, but sometimes his left knee wouldn't move much to his right on his backswing. Instead it would kick straight forward. That restricted his hip turn so he couldn't get his club, and himself, into position at the end of his backswing.

My left heel finally lifts, on my backswing, but that's something I just let happen. It's a result of swinging the club upward as I turn around my axis.

At the start of my downswing I replant my left heel. That starts everything in the other direction, so that my knees move to the left and my left side clears out of the way for my arms and club to follow.

Older people, especially those losing suppleness, need this sort of footwork. The less supple you are, the more good footwork will help you to make a full backswing turn. If you can get this full turn going back, it's much easier to turn in the opposite direction during your forward swing.

Just make sure that you don't start swinging forward before you've finished your backswing. My nephew, J.C., does this sometimes, and leaves his shots to the right as a result. That's when he could stand a little practice with his feet together, or barefooted, in waltz time.

Widen Your Arc
to Lengthen Your Shots

I've always enjoyed a sociable round of golf with friends, especially if there are a few dollars on the line. These days a $25 Nassau match suits me just fine. No one gets hurt; everyone keeps trying.

There was a time, though, when I'd find myself in matches involving thousands of dollars. It wasn't my money, of course. Some wealthy man would have me over to his club to be his partner in a match against two other high rollers. If we lost, my friend would pay. If we won, we'd split the take.

Twice in those matches, back in the 1930s, I happened to play against this man from New York. He was an outstanding amateur, probably one of the five best in the country. With about $10,000 on the line, my friend and I beat him and his partner both times.

When he paid off after the second match, in 1938, I remember him saying to me, "It's been enjoyable, Sam, but I hope I never meet you again on the golf course."

Last year we did finally meet again, on the practice range at a Florida club. We chatted a bit, and then I sat in a golf cart and watched him hit some shots.

His swing had become much shorter and faster. He was picking the club up with his right hand on his backswing and then throwing it sharply downward to the ball, even when it was sitting on a tee. His shots weren't going very far.

"Looks like you've shortened your swing," I said.

"I'm getting too old," he replied.

"You're not that old," I told him. Then I gave him some advice that I'm going to share with you.

Right away his drives started going about twenty yards farther.

"Boy, that feels good," he exclaimed. "Feels like shades of 1938."

It's only natural that a person's swing tends to get shorter with age, when we start to lose some of our flexibility. That's why most of the old-timers that still play well are those who started with long, fluid swings. Their strokes may be a bit shorter today, but they still create a long enough and wide enough arc to sweep the ball forward a pretty fair distance.

One big problem with a swing that starts getting too short and too narrow is that it also gets too steep. By that I mean that the clubhead gives the ball a blow that is too much downward and not enough forward. Too much of the force goes toward the ground instead of toward the target.

Naturally the downward blow reduces the length of shots, especially on drives where the ball is sitting on a tee. Most older golfers could increase their distance considerably by sweeping their shots off the peg.

The short, fast and narrow backswing also robs you of distance because your hands and arms end up doing almost all the work. The big muscles of your legs and back never get into the act.

As far as I'm concerned, the way you set up to the ball and start your backswing—the way you swing the club away from the ball for the first few inches—largely determines the width, length and speed of your overall swing. Thus your setup and takeaway pretty much decide whether you're going to sweep the ball forward or chop at it downward.

It helps to set up with more weight on your right foot than your left, with your right arm soft and your right hand light on the club.

This puts your weight behind the ball so you can sweep it forward. It also extends your left arm and puts your left side in control so you can make a wider swing arc.

From there you should make a forward press (see "Press Forward Before Starting Back") and then a takeaway that is (1) low, (2) slow and (3) straight back from the ball.

To make the clubhead start back low, you must sweep it along the ground with your left arm fully extended. This gives your swing a nice width, for maximum leverage. It brings your back muscles into play for extra power.

You won't get this leverage and power if you raise the club upward quickly with your right hand and arm. As soon as you pick the club up too fast, you cut off the turning of your body.

Starting the club back slow sets the pace for your swing. A slow start leads to a longer swing arc because you can continue to hold the club lightly. A fast start makes you increase your grip pressure to control the club. This tightening stifles the length of your backswing.

Starting the clubhead straight back from the ball—at least for a few inches—also helps extend the width of your swing. Moreover, it helps you sweep the ball away.

To sweep the ball forward, your clubhead must return to it from slightly inside your target line. That path gives it a nice shallow angle of approach.

The more it moves into the ball on a path from outside the target line, the steeper that angle of descent must be. That's when you get the downward chop.

I don't like to see people starting the club back to the inside—around themselves—too early in the takeaway. Then, if they get a bit too eager to hit the ball far, they'll react by shoving it outside the line on their downswing. Hence the chop.

So it's better at least to start the club back straight from the ball and then return it to impact from inside to along the target line.

I guess I've taken a lot of words to describe the first few inches of the swing, but I do feel they are extremely important. Just remember to make your takeaway LOW, SLOW and STRAIGHT.

If you can combine that type of takeaway with some good footwork (see "Use Your Feet for Extra Yards"), you'll take a few years off your swing and add more than a few yards to your drives.

17

It's Right to
Lead with Your Left

·In 1975 I was teaching golf in an adult instruction school sponsored by *Golf Digest* magazine. Early in the week I'd been out on the course, playing with the pupils and helping them with their swings and their strategy.

Then, later, I had a chance to watch these men and women on the practice range as they applied the instruction they'd received in their individual lessons.

Many of them were doing this strange thing as they swung the club. At first I thought they were hitting shots with only the left hand on the club. Then I realized that they were letting go with the right hand just after striking the ball.

The purpose of this drill was more or less to take the dominant right hand out of the shot, or at least to keep it in check. By thinking before-hand about releasing the right hand after impact, there was little chance that they could grab or throw with it during the downswing. Thus the left hand could pull the club into position and lead it slightly through the ball. It was really amazing how well these amateurs—many carried handicaps of 30 or higher—could contact the ball with only one hand in position during the follow-through. Most of them actually hit better shots than they did with both hands on the club throughout the swing.

Watching these people reinforced my own belief that most golfers tend to overuse their right hand as they swing. For left-handers, of course, it's the left hand that tends to dominate.

I can speak from personal experience too. For the last three or four years I've had tendonitis in my left wrist. Until it came on I suppose I played with my left hand in control as much as any right-hander ever could. But since then I've had to control my shots with my right hand and wrist.

This isn't nearly as effective. I'm sure it's a lot easier to pull something than it is to push it. I don't think you can control your shots as well with the right hand—your pushing, or throwing, hand—in charge. I know you can't hit the ball nearly as far. I also find it's more difficult to keep your balance.

The older golfer who wants a bit more distance would do well to increase his or her left-hand and left-side control, especially if he or she happens to be falling back onto the right foot during the follow-through. That's an almost certain sign that the right hand and right side have taken over at an earlier stage of the swing.

When the right hand takes over, it may flip the clubhead into the ball so that it outraces the left hand and arm. Throwing the club instead of swinging it can lead to a slowing down of the clubhead through impact. It also misaligns the clubface. This causes off-center, or glancing, blows and even less distance.

Sometimes the right hand closes the clubface so that the ball hooks wildly to the left. Or it may grab on tightly and keep the face from squaring in time. That's when you see shots slice to the right.

In either case it takes some sudden increase in right-hand grip pressure. Unfortunately, this is the natural thing for a normally right-handed person to do when he's trying to drive something a great distance.

I do think that the right hand has a job to do in the golf swing, but it should be a supporting role. The right hand is most effective when it sets on the club sort of passively throughout the backswing and until the last split second in the downswing. Then it can release some power and help out a bit, but to no greater extent than your left hand can control. The left hand and arm must continue to pace your swing, leading the clubhead through impact and somewhat beyond.

The whole thing boils down to either increasing your left hand's control or sublimating your right hand's influence, or both.

I'm afraid that the feeling of left-hand control isn't the easiest thing in the world to get across in a book. However, here are some key thoughts that can lead you into experiencing this sensation:

—Hold the club lightly in your right hand both before and throughout your swing.

—Retain control of the club in the last two fingers of your left hand, especially at the start of your downswing.

—Try to maintain this control by making your left arm and left side set the pace throughout your downswing. Keep pulling the club down and forward with your left arm and left side, so that your right hand, arm and side don't have a chance to push or throw it.

—Swing your left arm and the club freely THROUGH the ball, rather than AT it. This helps ensure that your left hand and arm keep moving forward, without your right hand's winning the race back to the ball.

"Heading"
for Extra Length

The first time I played golf with President Eisenhower he was having a bad day, particularly with his wood shots. Most of them were barely getting off the ground. Their lack of carry was costing him distance.

"Mr. President," I finally said as we stood on the tee of a long par-4 hole, "I've been watching you very closely. You don't turn enough on your backswing. That's why you're not getting your shots up."

With that he stood up to his ball, made a little bigger backswing and hit his best drive of the day.

"Sam," he said. "I don't know why it is; some days I outdrive everybody and other days I can't outdrive anybody."

On his second shot of the hole, he asked his caddie for his No. 2 wood. Again he made a full backswing. Again he flew the shot high and far. It landed just short of the green and finished next to the flagstick.

"You know my pro, Ed Dudley?" he then asked.

"Yes, sir."

"Well, he tells me the same thing you just said. 'Turn, turn, turn.' When I do, I usually hit good shots, but it's not easy for me to make a full turn."

The next time I played with the President, I noticed something unusual that helped explain why he was having trouble making a full turn on his backswing.

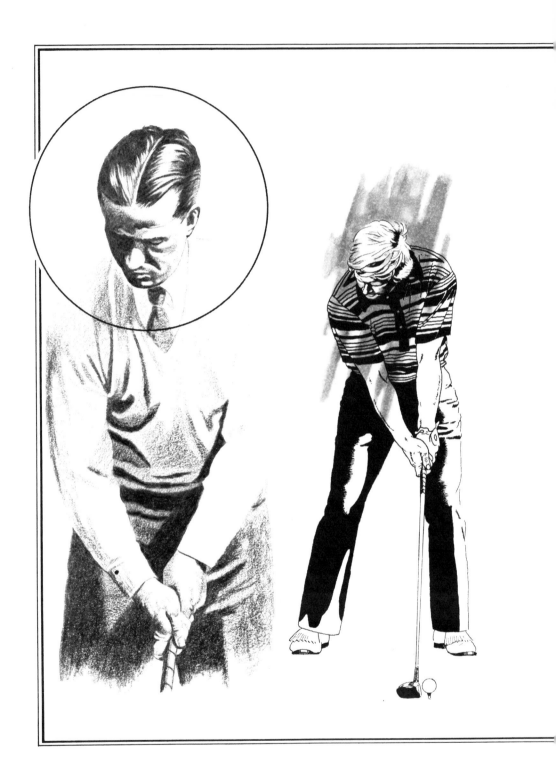

The problem started with his glasses. I noticed that they had fairly small frames.

You see, to make a full shoulder turn to the right during the backswing most people must also let their chin swivel or cock in that direction. If it doesn't, the neck muscles restrict the amount you can turn your shoulders. This restriction also cuts down on the amount you can swing your arms back and up and around. Indirectly it even restricts your hip turn.

Without a full backswing, most people chop down to the ball. The clubhead moves downward so steeply that it drives the ball forward too low. On drives where the ball is teed, you may chop under the ball and actually pop it high into the air, but not very far.

The President was having trouble letting his head swivel to the right. Whenever he did, he'd lose his view of the ball from within the small lenses of his glasses. This no doubt disconcerted him, at least subconsciously. Thus he'd fallen into the habit of holding his head rock-steady with his eyes glued to the ball. His frozen-head position was chopping off his backswing as surely as if he'd been playing golf with his neck in a plaster cast.

The President's physician, Dr. Paul Dudley White, happened to be with us. I told him of my diagnosis. He thought I was right, so I explained the situation to Ike. I suggested he get some glasses with extra-wide wraparound lenses.

He said he might try it, but I'm not sure that he ever did.

Almost all good players somehow get their chin cocked to the right so they can make a full backswing turn. Bobby Jones did it when he set up to the ball, well before he ever started his swing. Jack Nicklaus does it a little later, just a split second before he starts his takeaway. My head turns pretty much as part of my backswing.

But all three of us get it turned sooner or later, and all of us made or make backswings that are quite extensive.

If the older golfer needs anything, it's a backswing that's high, wide and handsome. He needs to give those old muscles every possible chance to function smoothly. He needs to get behind the ball during his backswing so he can really unload on his forward swing for maximum distance. Not making a full backswing in golf is like trying to pitch a baseball without rearing back first.

If you find that your backswing is getting shorter and shorter, or faster and faster, make sure that you cock your chin to your right before you start your swing. You'll be looking at the ball out of your left eye, if you're right-handed.

Also be sure that your head, in general, is positioned well behind the ball as you set up to swing. On a drive, with the ball opposite your left heel, your nose should be a good 8 to 10 inches behind it. This should make you feel as if most of your weight is on your right foot.

The only other thing you'll need to worry about as far as your head is concerned is that it stays more or less in that same general area throughout your swing. It should certainly stay at least that far behind the ball until you've made contact. Most good players' heads actually slide a bit farther to their right, and lower slightly, during their downswings.

You should keep your chin cocked to the right until you are well into your downswing. Thereafter you can, and should, allow it to naturally swivel back to the left as your arms swing into your follow-through.

These days you see many youngsters on the pro tour who coil themselves up like a corkscrew on the backswing. Their shoulders turn more than 90 degrees, while their hips turn hardly at all. This restricted hip turn may be fine for wasp-waisted, loose-jointed youngsters. We older players, however, need a full free backswing with everything moving in tandem—hips, shoulders and arms—as fully as possible. This is the best answer for fighting the battle of declining yardage. And all this free turning becomes a great deal easier when your head is screwed on correctly—cocked to the right—before you start.

Golf Magic—Turning
Pounds into Yards

There's a member at the club where I play in Florida who is typical of many older players. He's got what I call the "fat man's chop."

He stands no more than 5 feet 8 inches tall, but weighs at least 300 pounds. He loves the game, but is frustrated by a lack of length. Even his best drives seldom pass 150 yards.

Like so many people with big waistlines, this man slices his drives from left to right. Like most slicers, he's learned to avoid trouble on the right like a hound dog shuns skunks. He does it by aligning himself a good 50 degrees to the left, which is like trying to put out fire with a bucket of gasoline.

Aligning so far to the left sets him up to swing the clubhead back to the ball on an out-to-in path. The club will be cutting across his target line from right to left at impact, moving in the same direction he's aligned his whole body.

This out-to-in path makes the clubhead come down to the ball at a very steep angle—the fat man's chop—which is fine for hoeing weeds but not for driving golf balls forward. Too much force goes into the ground.

Also, with such a downward blow he can't really swing his arms freely and release his wrists into the shot. If he did, he'd stick his clubhead into the ground.

Since he can't do these things, it is almost impossible for him to square his clubface by the time it reaches the ball. It comes into impact facing to the right of target while moving to the left, which puts even more slice spin on the ball.

Thus he's losing distance on two counts. The open clubface gives him a glancing blow to the right, and his steep path downward applies most of what force he has toward the ground.

The problem is increased because he plays the ball far forward in his stance, well outside his left foot, which almost always happens when someone aligns so far to the left. This forward ball position puts his hands on the club in what is called a "weak" grip. Both hands are turned too far to the left at address. This makes it even more difficult for him to square the clubface by the time it reaches the ball. It gives his shots even more slice, and still fewer yards.

I told this man I could add forty yards to his drives in no time flat. The last time I saw him he said he was going to take me up on my offer. I hope he does.

The overweight golfer, especially an older person who's lost some flexibility, has everything going against him. The main thing is that he can't make a full turn on his backswing. There is simply too much flesh to move.

When you can't make a full backswing turn, it becomes very difficult to turn the other way on your forward swing. I know; I've had that same problem in recent years when I've also put on too much weight around the middle. Recently I've taken off twenty or so pounds and it makes all the difference.

Thus too much tummy can make it difficult to get anything into the shot except your arms and hands. That costs you distance.

A big waist even inhibits a free swinging of the arms. It gets in their way. You lose arm speed, and that also cuts down on yardage.

The fat person usually stands too far away from the ball. He must extend his arms over all that equator to make room for them to swing. Standing so far away makes you swing on a plane that is too flat. You must swing the club too much around yourself without enough upward movement of the club on the backswing. You lose some leverage, and more distance, as a result.

Or, instead of swinging too flat, the heavy golfer simply picks the club up with his hands and arms. It never gets far enough behind him to return to the ball from inside—his side—of the target line. Then he's got the fat man's chop, and the low slice from left to right.

Being forced to reach too far for the ball also creates tension in the arms and shoulders. This tension cuts off the length of the backswing and further inhibits free movement of the arms and wrists.

The big stomach can make balance a problem. It forces you to take a stance that's too wide, which further restricts a free turning of the hips. It makes your arms and shoulders do all the work.

I could go on and on about the troubles of the overweight golfer, but it's time to start coming up with some solutions. Obviously the first and best answer is simply to lose weight. Short of that, however, there are some other things that will help. If you tend to slice most of your long shots—you may occasionally pull one to the left on a straight line—or if you pull your short irons to the left, I advise you try what I suggest. The same would be true if you sometimes pop your drives high into the air or scoot them along the ground to the left, or if you often feel like you've "looked up." All of these results are symptomatic of the fat man's chop.

First you should understand that your goal is to sweep your shots forward. That goal demands that your clubhead move into the ball on a path that is from your side of the target line, not from out beyond it. The inside path will help give your clubhead a shallower approach into the ball. It will send the force of the blow forward instead of downward.

You must address the ball in a way that will let you swing the clubhead into it on this path. You may need to align your shoulders—but not your feet—more to the right than you have been. You may need to play the ball a bit farther back in your stance, a bit inside your left heel.

See where your shots start out. If they still start out to the left—

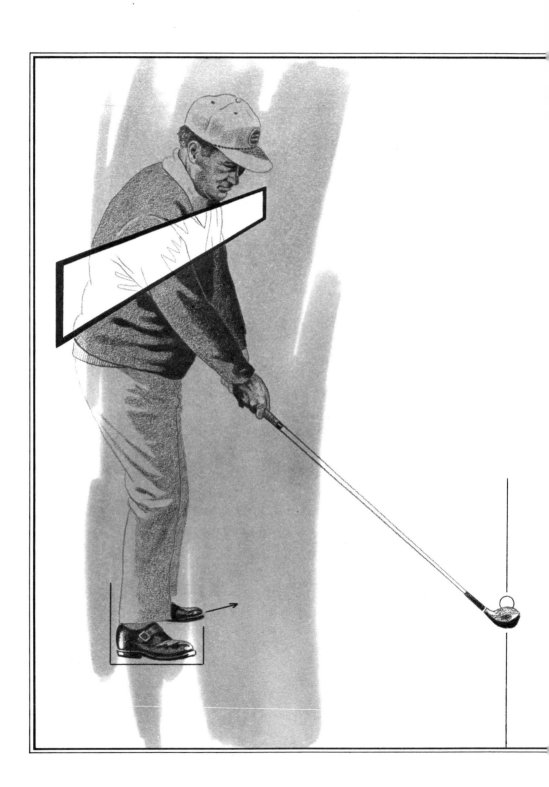

regardless of where they curve to after that—you're still not getting that clubhead moving from inside to along the line. Visualize that path before you swing and keep trying to swing back to the ball along it.

Another thing to do before you swing is to start with more weight on your right foot. One big problem of the overweight golfer is moving out of his own way on his downswing. His left side never turns clear in time for his arms to swing freely forward. It helps to start with more weight on the right side at address. Then it's much easier to shift and turn to the left during the downswing. If your weight doesn't get to the right in the backswing, it can't move to the left when you shift directions.

Aligning the shoulders more to the right at address, along with setting more weight on the right foot, makes it easier for heavy golfers to make a full backswing turn. The full turn puts the club into a position at the top of the swing from where you can get at the ball from inside the target line.

Once you've turned fully, however, you must swing the club freely downward and forward with your arms. Give it a good swish.

In summary, set up to the ball so you can make a full backswing and swish the clubhead into the ball from inside to along your target line.

Beyond that, here are some additional tips that will help most older, overweight golfers who tend to slice their long shots from left to right and pull the short ones to the left.

—Hold the club lightly at address and keep it light throughout the swing.

—Hold the club more in the fingers of your left hand.

—Toe out the left foot to the left, more toward the target.

—Narrow the width of the stance.

—Be sure to make a forward press.

—Make a longer, slower backswing.

—Try to point the clubshaft toward the target at the top of the backswing, rather than off to the left. Again, hold it lightly.

Obviously you can't think about all these things at the same time. Pick one or two and work on them in your practice sessions. Just keep working to create as much freedom of arms and body motion as you can, and to swing the clubhead into the ball from inside—your side—of the target line.

Finally, I suggest you follow this simple drill. At every meal, before dessert is served, place both hands firmly against the edge of the table and push yourself backward and upward, with a full extension of both arms.

Improving Your
Short Game

Make the Chip
Your Money Shot

Paul Bunyan is a fictional giant of the logging industry, a Gulliverlike strongman who chopped down trees like you'd snap toothpicks.

Paul Runyan is no giant of fiction or anything else. He's a small, slight man who succeeded as a professional golfer despite an amazing lack of length on his shots.

Between these two Pauls, Bunyan would have driven it past Runyan at golf like Stirling Moss past Grandma Moses at Le Mans.

But Runyan would have beaten Bunyan—somehow, some way. That's why they called him "Little Poison." That's why he's my all-time choice as the golfer who got the most out of the least.

I felt like Bunyan when I played Runyan in the finals of the 1938 PGA Championship at Shawnee, Pennsylvania. My drives usually finished fifty yards, or more, past his. On one long, par-5 hole, my first two shots went farther than his first three.

But Runyan beat this Bunyan. He did it largely with an amazing exhibition around the greens. Paul would sink a shot from behind a bush, or chip dead to the cup time and again. He dropped a putt of sixty feet from off the green. Once my ball came to rest on the green directly between his and the hole. For the second time in the tournament I became subject to the stymie rule then in effect. He wedged his over mine and into the cup—on the fly.

The end result was Runyan over Snead, 8 holes up with 7 to play.

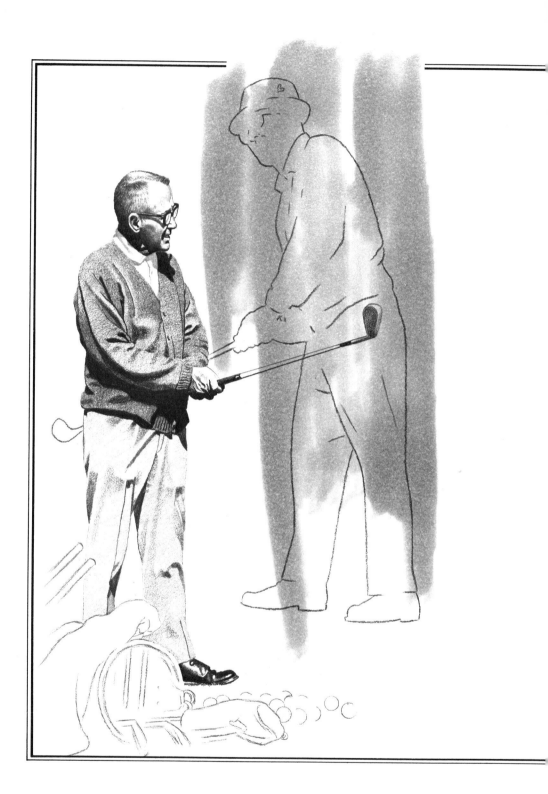

It turned out to be the worst final-round licking in the thirty-nine years that the PGA was a match-play event.

All golfers could do with a bit of Runyan's chipping magic. Probably those who need it most, however, are players who are losing distance off the tees or getting too nervous on the greens. I suspect that most golfers over forty fit into one or both of those categories.

If you're getting shorter on tee shots, you're probably starting to miss more greens on approach shots. Naturally, that means you're going to be chipping more of the time. Your chipping, good or bad, will largely determine whether or not those shorter drives are going to mean higher scores.

If you're starting to tense up on some of your putts, you'll find that good chipping saves you a lot of misery. I can say from personal experience that it sure is comforting when most of your run-up shots are finishing within two or three feet of the hole instead of six, eight or ten feet. Those 10-footers can look like 10-yarders when you need one to save an important par.

Here are some thoughts that I think will help you turn those 10-footers into 2-footers:

—Look on chip shots as if they were long putts. Choke down on the club to about putter-length and stroke largely with your arms. You don't need to complicate your motion with wrist and body action unless it's an unusually long chip.

—Set most of your weight on your left foot and keep it there throughout your stroke. This gives you a slightly DOWNWARD-moving clubhead into and through the ball for crisp, solid contact. Never try to lift, scoop, flip or otherwise help the ball fly upward; usually you'll dig in behind it or catch only its top part with your blade.

—Keep your grip pressure constant throughout your stroke. This takes some trying for a while, but it helps make your shots go the right distance.

—Land the ball on the green whenever you can.

—Get it rolling on the green as soon as you can. The free-running chip is safer and more accurate than the high, soft pitch shot.

Finally, I suggest that you older golfers spend a lot of time learning to make all sorts of short shots with the same club, rather than one basic shot with many different clubs. Take an 8-iron, say, and learn to hit shots that are short and long, high and low, soft and hot, from good lies and tight lies, and so on.

I know one old-timer who may miss eleven or twelve greens and still shoot only one or two over par. He uses the same club—a sand iron— on every shot he has around the green. I mean he can make that club talk, sing, whistle and hum. You name the key; he's got the shot. He's also got a small piece from a lot of people's wallets.

A New Putter
Soothes Twitching Nerves

I remember hearing Bobby Jones saying to Tommy Armour, "You know, I once brushed in those 4, 5 and 6-foot putts with no problem. Now I'm leaving them to the right, the left, too short, too long."

"You've got 'em, Bob," Armour replied.

"Got what?"

"You've got the bloody yips. And once you've got 'em, you never lose 'em."

It's true. During my career of some forty years in pro golf, I've gotten the yips four times. And I don't mean in just four different rounds, or tournaments. I mean for a run of months, or even years.

They call them the "yips," but I prefer the British term, "twitches." For me they started with a feeling of tension in my stomach. It would tie up into a knot. Then the tension would start spreading all over, into my chest, down my arms and, finally, to the tips of my fingers.

The twitches are born from a lack of confidence, a fear of missing the putt. That's why they break out most frequently on those short putts that you and everyone else expects you to make.

They hit older people especially because their nerves have become a bit frayed with the passing of time. Suddenly, somewhere during the stroke, those nerves go crazy. They become impossible to control. So does your stroke. The ball goes everywhere, except into the hole.

Some days they aren't so bad. Other times, especially when the

greens are unusually fast or when the stakes seem extra important, they start to grab you every time you take the putter out of the bag.

My worst case of the twitches started in late 1946 when I played Bobby Locke a series of sixteen matches in his native South Africa.

Locke is without doubt one of the three best putters in the history of the game. He has always used an old hickory-shafted blade putter, and the most unorthodox technique you could imagine. He aligns his feet and body so far to the right that he looks like he is going to stroke the ball off that side of the green. Actually, it's the same alignment he uses on his full shots, which he invariably hooks into his target from right field. But I've never seen a man drop so many 30- and 40-footers.

Locke beat me so badly on those South African greens that I won only two of the sixteen matches. Two others I managed to tie. Later he came to America and did the same sort of damage to our PGA circuit players.

My confidence in putting was so shattered that in one match I actually missed eight putts that were no longer than the club I had in my hand.

After I returned to the States, my twitches laid me low for over two years. I'd won six PGA tour events in 1946, plus the British Open. I didn't win a thing in 1947. My earnings were only $9,703. In 1948 they dropped to $6,980. In many rounds I used up more strokes on the greens than I took to reach them.

In early 1949 I returned to the tour after a winter of working on my putting at the Greenbrier. In my first event, the Tucson Open, I finished in eighteenth place. The twitches were still there.

When I went to clear out my locker after the tournament, I noticed this putter that someone had left in it. The club had a used look about it, but it felt good in my hands. The shaft felt fairly stiff when I waggled it. Overall it seemed heavier than normal, probably about sixteen ounces. Its straight-faced head was made of brass, and the shaft entered it near center. It looked like an easy putter to aim.

At the time no one knew who owned the putter, but later Stan Kertes, a Chicago pro, came up to me at the Greensboro Open and said it was his. I hadn't planned to use the club, but Stan didn't seem to want it either. He told me to keep it for a while.

On a hunch, I used the Kertes putter at Greensboro—and won. I dropped putts that seemed to cover half of North Carolina. My confidence in my putting returned at Greensboro as quickly as it had vanished in South Africa.

The next week at the Masters, after the second round, I went to the practice green and again started sinking everything, from any distance. My final rounds of 67–67 assured me that with Stan's putter I could once again handle pressure on the greens. I needed only thirty putts the final day, and dropped a curling 9-footer on the last green for my first title at Augusta.

From there I went on to win the PGA Championship, the Western Open and several other events. At one stage I shot 69 or better in 22 of 24 rounds. They named me "Golfer of the Year."

In 1950 I set a postwar record that still stands, winning nine tournaments. With the Kertes putter I finished in the money in sixty-two straight tournaments. I didn't yip a putt.

Then, one day in 1952, my assistant at the Greenbrier, Eddie Thompson, leaned a bit too hard on my putter. It snapped in two where the shaft entered the head. Shortly after that the twitches started bothering me once again. Like Armour said, once you've got them you never lose them, at least not for good.

I believe that confidence is 90 percent of putting. A putter that makes you feel secure over a sliding 4-footer for all the marbles is like having a sure tee time beyond the Pearly Gates.

As I say, the twitches seem to get you when you're older, yet I still see older golfers twitching with putters they've used since childhood. It just doesn't make sense to me.

Don't think there's anything sacred about your putter just because it worked for you as a teen-ager. If it doesn't give you the security you need to make a smooth stroke under pressure, I suggest you apply for a divorce and start looking for a new mate.

I suggest you look for one that's slightly on the heavy side. It seems that twitching goes hand in hand with a putter that's too light. Perhaps it's because you can't feel the head so well on a light putter. Maybe it's because you require a longer stroke than you'd otherwise need.

I also suggest you seek a putter that you find easy to aim, and one that soles flat on the ground when your hands are in a comfortable position. Beyond these guidelines, I'll leave the choice up to you.

But try several putters before you make a final choice. Your club professional no doubt has a good selection on hand, and he'll let you try as many as you wish. If he doesn't, or if you can't find what you're looking for, just go down the road to another pro shop.

I don't mean to say that you can't regain confidence on the greens by improving your technique. In the chapters that follow I'll tell you some ways to make that better, too. But all the technique in the world isn't likely to pay off in the long run with a putter that's given you nightmares in the past.

Stick with the Line
You've Got in Mind

We've all had certain putts that stand out in our memory. For me, one of these is a sidehill 3-footer on the final green during the 1959 Sam Snead Festival tournament at the Greenbrier. It was a putt that I needed for a 59 and my lowest score ever in competition.

I'd just missed a 6-footer for a birdie on 17 and had come to the last hole a bit irritated. Then I said to myself, "Well, you shouldn't be too unhappy when you've got a tournament in your pocket and a 60 if you can make one more par."

With that I hit a very good drive into a pretty strong wind. A crisp 5-iron shot left me with the short right-to-left putt.

But as I looked and looked at the upcoming putt, I started finding more ways to miss it than Colonel Sanders has chicken legs. It looked like it didn't break too much. It looked like it broke a lot. It looked slow, then fast. I imagined it spinning around the high side of the cup and finishing four or five feet below it. I saw it missing on the left.

My amateur partner was saying, "Who's away? Whose turn to putt?" and I kept thinking of ways to make mine miss the hole.

Finally I said to him, "Let me get this thing over with. In ten seconds there won't even be a hole to putt at."

I stepped up to the putt, aimed a bit to the right of the hole to allow for the break and started my backstroke.

Then, at the last split second, I hit the ball with a little extra force.

The ball broke more to the left than I'd expected, but it still caught the bottom half of the hole and toppled in for my 59. Without that extra force I'd given my stroke, I surely would have left the ball below the cup.

I was lucky on that putt. I'd changed my mind in midstream and still found the cup. Usually it doesn't work that way. Indecision usually leads to disaster.

For instance, in the 1947 U.S. Open at St. Louis Country Club I needed to sink a 30½-inch left-to-right putt on the final green to tie Lew Worsham in our playoff for the title. I decided to allow for about three inches of break. Then I changed my mind, because maybe the putt wouldn't curve that much. It did. I missed the putt, and lost the Open, by the exact amount of curve I'd decided at the last second that I didn't need.

It seems that as a general rule the older we get, the less positive we become about our putting. As youngsters we seldom considered missing a putt. The hole was something to roll the ball into.

As the years pass, however, we start seeing every putt as a breaking putt, even when the green is, in fact, billiard-table flat. We begin to anticipate missing instead of making.

For many older players this indecision results simply from a growing difficulty in reading putts. Late in his career, I played Henry Cotton, the great British pro who dominated European golf from the mid-1930s to about 1950. Not once during that round did Henry even make the effort to read a putt. He left that chore to his caddie, who would do the lining up and then would tell Cotton where to aim—two inches left, three inches right or whatever. Actually it worked quite well for Henry.

The point I'm making is that indecision about your putting line leads to an indecisive putting stroke. Read your putts carefully. Pay particular attention to the area around the hole. That's where the putt will be slowing down, where gravity will have its greatest effect in pulling the ball down a slope.

Also, if you don't already size up your putts from the side as well as from behind the ball, I suggest you build that habit into your pre-putt routine. The side view not only helps clarify the direction a putt will break, but also helps you get a feeling for the length it needs to roll.

But once you see the line that you want your putt to follow, stick with it. Once you've actually set the club behind the ball and aimed it down that path, forget about direction. Put it out of your mind once and for all. Concentrate solely on stroking the ball the correct distance.

Stroke Long Putts
Close, Short Putts In

I really had not wanted to play in the 1946 British Open. First prize was only $600. I'd lose even if I won.

And winning wasn't likely. I'd been putting like a gorilla in boxing gloves.

Also, I knew that I couldn't use my center-shafted putter in the event. The British had barred that type after Walter Travis beat them with his center-shafted Schenectady model in their 1904 Amateur. I didn't relish the changeover to a heel-shafted blade.

But L. B. Icely, the president of Wilson Sporting Goods Company, changed my mind. Wilson was paying me good money to endorse Sam Snead golf equipment, and Mr. Icely felt that a big overseas victory would greatly improve my prestige. He also pointed out that the huge greens at St. Andrews might help me regain my putting touch.

The Old Course at St. Andrews is fairly unique in that six of the greens serve as a putting surface for two different holes. They place two cups in each so that, for instance, the second-hole green is also the 16th, the third the 15th, the fourth the 14th, and so on.

These double greens are so big that sometimes you almost need binoculars to see the hole. Putts of 125 feet or more are common. And in 1946, before they installed a watering system, these greens were so hard and fast that a strong wind could actually blow the ball from a standing position.

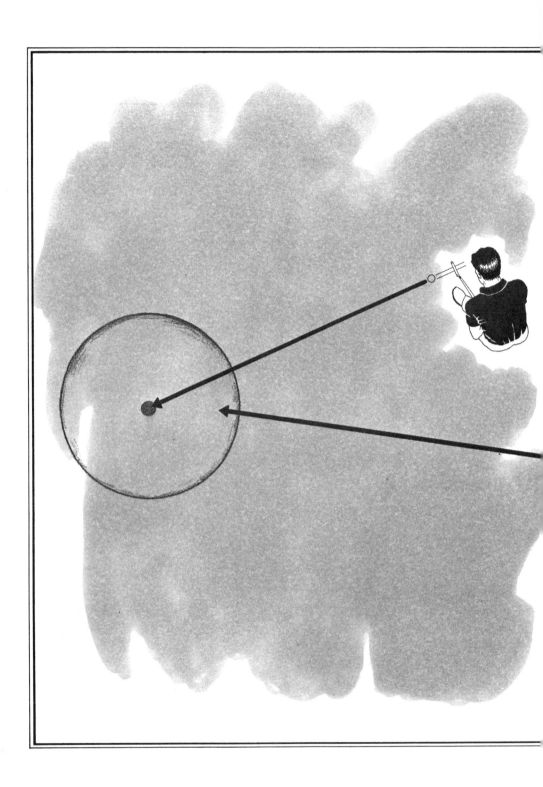

Before the tournament started, my caddie pointed out to me where the holes were likely to be cut for the competition.

"How do you know they'll put it there?" I asked on one particular hole.

"Because that's where they've put it for fifty years," he replied.

After learning where they would put the pins on those huge slick greens, I realized that Old Sam just might have a chance to win the Open. I figured that since no one would sink many putts, everyone would be reduced to my level on the greens. Maybe I could putt the rest of the boys to a stand-off and beat them with my tee-to-green game.

I decided then and there that I'd never try to sink a long putt. My only goal would be to lag the ball close enough for a reasonably easy second putt.

My strategy paid off. I went into the final round tied for the lead. That day the wind blew so hard that balls were jiggling when you stood up to putt. You didn't dare ground your putter for fear the ball would blow away and cost you a stroke. On one hole Flory Van Donck, the Belgian pro, had a downhill 20-footer with the wind. He turned his back to the hole and actually nudged the ball in the opposite direction, uphill. The ball ran up and into the wind a foot or two and then reversed course back toward the cup. It passed the hole without even saying "goodbye" and finished ten feet on the low side.

I had one downhiller myself. I tapped the ball so gently that I was able to walk to the hole before the ball arrived. As soon as it stopped next to the cup, I tapped it in, before it had a chance to blow away.

The only green I three-putted on the final nine was the 16th, where someone had stuck the cup just beyond an uphill slope. My first try up the slope didn't quite reach the top. The ball rolled back a good twenty-five feet to where I was standing. I made the slope on my next putt, however, and tapped in for a bogey-5.

I continued my policy of lagging first putts, however. On the 17th I gave my 25-footer just enough steam to finish at the hole. It took a few extra turns in the wind and plopped in. That cinched the tournament.

Since that day I've always played long putts to finish NEAR the hole and short putts IN the hole. Generally speaking, I won't try to sink anything over twenty feet. All I do is aim on line and then try to make the ball die at the cup.

Only on the shorter putts will I put enough speed on the ball to make it pass the hole if it should miss.

The old saying, "never up, never in," is obviously true, but I think it's a bad philosophy, especially for any older players whose aging nerves may be making them a bit shaky on 3- and 4-footers. Trying to sink long putts frequently sends the ball that distance, or farther, past the hole. Then you've got a problem.

When you really analyze why people three-putt, it's obvious that misdirection is not the major problem. Most everyone can read a green and putt more or less on line most of the time.

It's misjudging length that kills you, finishing several feet short or long of the hole. If most players could make every putt finish hole-high they'd very seldom, if ever, take three putts.

If three-putting is costing you strokes, I suggest you take into account how many times your first try finished too short or too long. That analysis should convince you to putt those long ones to the hole with distance being your only consideration as you make your stroke.

You'll be surprised how many times you actually sink a long putt, even though your goal was merely to finish close to the hole.

The cut-off distance where you decide to sink instead of lag will vary from day to day and with the type of putt you happen to face. Some days you are more confident that you can make short putts if you happen to miss the hole on your first attempt. But you'd be more likely to lag your first try if the greens were unusually slick, or if the cup were set in an area where the ball might run on and on beyond the hole.

In any case, on long putts plan where you want your ball to finish if you should miss. Aim on a line that you think will take it into the cup, but then forget about direction and focus strictly on rolling the putt with just enough speed to make it die within tap-in range.

Arm Putting
Reduces Wrist Twitching

Early in my golfing career I was a "wrist putter." There was relatively little arm motion back and forward in my stroke. My wrists simply cocked on the backstroke and uncocked on my forward stroke.

This wristiness is obvious in early photos of me on the greens. Except on very long putts, my left forearm rests firmly against my side throughout my sroke. It never moves forward with the putterhead on my follow-through.

Wrist putting was the style of the times, shown at its best in the stroke of Bobby Jones. Generally speaking, you still see more wristiness in the putting strokes of golfers who developed their games, say, before World War II, than you do in the modern players.

Wrist putting worked quite well for me until the mid-1940s. I believe I was excellent on very long putts, where my arms did, necessarily, come into play. I was also quite good on those 10- and 12-footers where the wrists did all the work.

Gradually, however, I started missing putts inside twelve feet more and more frequently. It got so I was a little better from twenty feet than I was from six.

The twitches had taken over. They hit me so badly in one tournament, the Los Angeles Open, that on one putt of eighteen inches I jabbed the ball two feet past the cup. Then I jerked the next one, too—three putts from less than two feet!

After that I decided that wrist putting had to go. It didn't stand up under pressure. I couldn't control those nerves and muscles in my fingers and hands. As soon as I started stroking a short putt that I knew I was supposed to make easily, the club would go off in my hands like a rattlesnake striking its prey.

I left the tour for a while to try and figure things out. I needed a way to move the putter back and through, even under pressure, without relying on those small, lightning-quick muscles in my hands and fingers.

One thing I discovered was that I could immobilize my wrists by holding the club with a very tight grip. Not only did this freeze my wrists, so that only my arms could move the putter back and through, but it also made sure that my grip pressure didn't increase during my stroke. I couldn't tighten it because it was already so tight.

In the past I'd always held the putter lightly in my hands, just as on the other shots. I'd start with a light grip and try to keep it light throughout my stroke. But when the twitches started getting to me, this light grip would loosen even more on my backstroke and then clamp down before I struck the ball. The clamping ruined everything—my rhythm, the path of the putterhead and the direction in which it was facing.

The tight grip worked, at least for a while. In the first tournament I used it, the Goodall Round Robin on Long Island, I played five matches and only three-putted one green. I didn't make too many putts over ten feet, but at least I didn't embarrass myself on the short ones. It worked well enough for me to win the event.

Today you see these young pros on the PGA tour using strokes that are almost entirely a pendulum movement of the arms with little or no wrist action. The left arm keeps moving toward the hole so that the right hand doesn't have a chance to flip the clubhead forward and misalign the aim of the putterface.

I think arm putting is far more reliable under pressure. Billy Casper is about the only really good putter I can think of who still taps the ball forward with his hands and wrists. I guess Billy has found some sort of peace of mind that lets him get away with that type of stroke.

Because the arms are less likely to twitch than the hands and wrists, I suggest arm putting for older golfers who might be having trouble on the greens because of bad nerves.

Actually, arm putting is a better method even if your nerves are still in good shape. When the arms sweep the putter back and forward, the putterhead stays lower to the ground at each end of the stroke. It moves back and through on a shallower path than when the wrists cock it upward on the backstroke and then again on the follow-through.

Also, arm putting sends the ball forward a bit more "quietly" off the putterface. It doesn't jump off so quickly as when the wrists come into play. I think that this gentler starting of the putt makes it easier to control the distance that the ball will travel.

If you try arm putting, first practice stroking putts with just your left hand on the club—right hand if you are left-handed. This will gradually give you the feeling of moving your left arm away from your side and down the line on your follow-through, a movement that you will not have made in the past as a wrist putter. Putting with only one hand on the club also forces you to develop a smooth rhythm, which is vital to all putting, but especially when stroking with the arms.

As far as grip pressure is concerned, I think it's best to hold the club lightly if you can retain that lightness throughout your stroke under pressure situations. The light grip gives you a bit more feel.

However, if your nerves don't let you keep it light throughout, then start with a tightened grip and keep it firm all the way. You may sacrifice a bit of feel, but at least your fingers and wrists won't throw or grab the putter in midstroke.

Finally, don't fall into the trap of worrying about making an arm stroke when you are playing on the course. It's very difficult to sink putts when you're thinking about how to make your stroke. Instead, develop that habit of arm stroking through practice. Build it into your muscle memory. Gradually it will become part of your technique on the course. It will start to happen automatically without any mental effort on your part.

My Final Answer—
Sidesaddle Putting

I blew past my fiftieth birthday in 1962, barely taking time to snuff out the candles on my cake. The pro tour had grown to almost $2 million in annual prize money—about twenty times more than when I'd started a quarter century earlier. I'd won the World Cup individual title in 1961, plus the Sam Snead Festival and the Tournament of Champions, and I figured to collect a few more coins in the years to come.

Besides, I was having fun bumping heads with a whole new generation of golfers—Palmer, Casper, Player, Littler, and a youngster who'd just jumped on the carousel, a kid named Nicklaus. It was no time to leave the party.

Twelve years later in 1974, my thirty-seventh as a touring pro, I won more money than ever before—over $55,000. I was sixty-two at the time, old enough to be a granddaddy to many of the youngsters I was outscoring.

Looking back I'm sure I'd never have lasted except for an incident that happened in the 1966 PGA Championship. I'd led the field after the first two days, but then on the 10th green of the third round my hands jerked in the middle of my putting stroke. I actually hit the ball twice on the same putt.

The twitches were back. I sensed then and there that I'd better do something to combat my nerves. If I didn't, it would be out to pasture for Old Sam.

On the next green I set up to the putt like you would in croquet, with your feet straddling the ball. I ran my right hand about halfway down the puttershaft. Then I used that arm only to move the putterhead back and forward. The ball fell into the cup.

I did the same thing on the next two holes. Both putts dropped.

Don January, my playing partner, shook his head and said, "Hell, Sam, why don't you putt that way all the time?"

I did just that, and it worked. By moving the putter back and forward with only my right arm and shoulder doing the work, I was arm putting to the nth degree. It was impossible for those nerves in my wrist and fingers to twitch because they never moved independently of the arm itself.

Then one day I heard the bad news. The United States Golf Association had just ruled that straddling the line when putting would be illegal. I was crushed. It looked like I was finished, unless I could find a way to sidestep the new rule.

That's exactly what I did. I remembered an old-timer I'd seen over in England several years before. He must have been in his seventies at the time, but he would bet that he could outputt anyone. And he'd done pretty well, too, with a takeoff on the style I'd just been banned from using.

This man had putted the same way I was, facing the hole, but he hadn't straddled the line. Instead he'd placed his right foot next to his left and putted the ball from off his right side—sidesaddle.

It didn't take me long to get the hang of this style. Actually, as a youngster I'd spent hours on end pitching horseshoes with my uncle behind the barn on our farm. I just put more or less that same movement into my putting. It's kept me going ever since.

At first there were those who chuckled at my strange way of putting. Maybe some still do, but I haven't heard them. I know that many of the men I played against in the 1930s and 1940s wish they could still compete in the PGA Seniors tournament, but they never show up. They've got the twitches, and too much pride to try something so unconventional as sidesaddle putting.

It's as I once said to the late Bobby Jones after he remarked to me that sidesaddle was "a hell of a way to putt."

"Well, Bob," I answered, "when you come in off the course they don't ask you how. They ask you how many."

If you've got the twitches and they keep coming back no matter what you try, you might wish to experiment with sidesaddle putting. It works because it takes all the burden of moving the putter away from your fingers and wrists. The right arm does all the work, and it never bends at the elbow. It's nothing more than an appendage to the putter itself.

There are other advantages too. I think it's easier to see the putting line, and to move the putter back and forward along it, when you're facing in that direction. It's also easier to contact the ball exactly on the sweetspot of the putterface time after time.

And it's easier to keep the putterhead accelerating forward, as you should with any putting style. You're less likely to "quit" on the stroke because, again, you're moving the club in the same direction you're facing.

I find that center-shafted putters work better than the malletheads or the heel-shafted blades. It also feels more comfortable if you've got a piece of grip around the shaft about midway down, where you hold on with your right hand, or if you extend your club's regular grip down to that area. Most club professionals can modify your putter in either of those ways.

Beyond that, the main points to stress are your grip, address position and stroke. After years of experimenting, here are the things that I recommend:

Hold the top of the club in your left hand just as you would the stickshift on the floor of a car if it were on your left side. Lay your thumb over the top end of the club, pointing it toward the hole, and wrap your fingers around the grip.

Set your right palm behind the middle of the shaft so that the palm faces in the same direction as the putterface. The shaft should extend across the base of your forefinger and upward between the thumb and heel pads of your palm. Lay your thumb lightly over the front of the shaft, gently pressing the club against your forefinger and palm. Keep this thumb pressure consistently light throughout your stroke.

Stand to the left of the ball with your feet together and angled slightly off to the left. Your right toe should sit a few inches forward of your left.

Play the ball about three inches ahead of your right toe—slightly farther on long putts—and just far enough away from your right side so that you won't club your foot during your backstroke.

Flex your knees and bend forward from your hips as you set the putterhead behind the ball facing directly down your intended line. Your right arm should hang straight downward, but it should not be rigid. Your left arm should be bent about 90 degrees at the elbow with the upper arm close to your side and the forearm pointing forward, parallel to your putting line.

Your eyes should face directly down your intended line and be positioned directly over it. This means you'll need to lean your upper body a bit to the right.

I find that I put a better roll on the ball if I catch it with a slightly downward stroke. Thus I tilt the top of my putter shaft a bit forward, toward the target, before I begin my stroke.

The stroke itself is nothing more than a pendulum movement, back and forward, with only the straight right arm and shoulder doing any work. It's nothing more than a rhythmical movement of the putterhead in the direction you wish the ball to roll.

The left hand stays in place and acts only as a hinge for the butt end of the putter. Only on very long putts should it move back and forward slightly.

Be sure to look only at the ball as you stroke, but keep the hole in your mind's eye. This will help greatly in rolling the ball in the right direction and the right distance.

Above all, avoid any right-hand wrist action. Do it all with the arm and shoulder.

At first sidesaddle putting may seem somewhat awkward, but with a half hour or so of practice it will begin to feel natural and pay dividends. You may begin to wonder, as I have, why we ever started putting "conventionally" in the first place.

My Final Word—
Play More, Enjoy More

Back in 1965 I was on safari in Africa. We were out there in the bush shooting mostly elephant and buffalo, and I was loving every minute of it.

Golf was the farthest thing from my mind, except for once when I started calculating how long it had been since I'd taken a vacation from the game. I figured that I'd either practiced or played golf for thirteen straight years without so much as a two-week break.

The next thing I knew, there came a call over the radio from some people in Nairobi. They wanted me to come and play an exhibition match.

I told them "no."

"I didn't bring my clubs," I explained. "I didn't bring my shoes. I didn't bring anything pertaining to golf."

But the voice on the radio kept insisting that I had to play this exhibition.

Finally I said I'd do the exhibition. My fee was to be five leopard skins.

I played a match against their two best amateurs and tied their better-ball score. I used borrowed clubs and wore an old pair of suede street shoes, which started rubbing against my feet soon after we'd started.

I knew I had to do something to prevent my feet from blistering

because the bacteria over there are something fierce; a blister could turn into a festering sore by nighttime.

I decided to free up my feet by cutting away part of the shoes with a knife. By the time I'd finished the round I had nothing left except the soles and part of the toes. My feet were sore; my heels were blistered.

When it came time for me to collect my leopard skins, it turned out they didn't have five—only three. One of them wasn't much bigger than a house cat. So much for my vacation from golf.

Later I tried to get away another time, again on safari in Africa. This time one of my friends, Gordon Fawcett, had brought along a couple of clubs, but no balls.

How does one play golf without balls in the African bush? Simple. Dig a hole in the ground for a target and then gather up some elephant droppings—make sure they are well-dried—for ammunition.

You can't hit these "balls" too hard because they will explode, but I did find a way to win the match. By making sure that I always hit my dropping on its hardest side, I'd finish the hole with it still intact. Gordon's kept falling apart.

When it all started I never dreamed I'd still be playing some 250 rounds of golf per year at age sixty-five. But therein lies whatever "secret" there may be to playing the game fairly well later in life. My game would never have held together nearly as well as it has if I'd taken so much as even one year's hiatus. I think that golf is the most difficult game to play well. Most surely it is the most difficult when you play infrequently.

So my final advice in this book is simply that you play as much golf as you possibly can, and that you practice those things that are most important to your particular game. Hopefully I've told you some things that will help you shoot lower scores and, therefore, become inspired to play with even greater frequency.

Above all, I hope that this book somehow adds to your enjoyment of this wonderful game that we share, and that we can sit down and chat about it should our future paths happen to cross.

Index